TO

FROM

DATE

KEVIN WEATHERBY

COME & SEE

COWBOY DEVOTIONS

TO STRENGTHEN YOUR RIDE WITH CHRIST

DaySpring

Come & See: Cowboy Devotions to Strengthen Your Ride with Christ

First Edition, February 2024

Published by:

DaySpring

Published by DaySpring, 501 Nelson Place, Nashville, TN 37214, USA. DaySpring is an imprint of HarperCollins Christian Publishing, Inc.

Unless otherwise noted, all Scripture quotations are taken from The Simplified Cowboy Version, which is NOT a Bible translation. It was never intended to be a Bible, nor should it be thought of as such. The SCV is a Bible paraphrase intended to merely catch a glimpse of the Bible's deep wisdom, and most importantly, to see Jesus Christ through the eyes of a working ranch cowboy. Kevin Weatherby's hope is that the words in this paraphrase will lead you deep into the real Word of God.

DaySpring titles may be purchased in bulk for educational, business, fundraising, or sales promotional use. For information, please email SpecialMarkets@ThomasNelson.com.

HarperCollins Publishers, Macken House, 39/40 Mayor Street Upper, Dublin 1, D01 C9W8, Ireland (https://www.harpercollins.com)

Written by: Kevin Weatherby
Cover Design by: Greg Jackson

ISBN: 979-8-88602-398-5

Printed in China
26 27 28 29 30 CPP 7 6 5 4 3

Contents

Introduction to the Simplified Cowboy Version

Around 2009, I was the pastor of a small cowboy church in West Texas. Our church was doing the concession stand at the local high school rodeo. We also had a little booth where we gave away some free Bibles as well as information about our church. While everyone else was working the concession stand, I worked the booth.

The dad of one of the rodeo contestants walked up and eyed the Bibles. He picked one up and asked if it was a cowboy Bible. I told him that it was one of the easier translations to read. I offered it to him to take home. What happened next changed my life.

He said, "I've got a lot of those 'easier to read' translations at the house. Just because someone puts a cowboy on the cover, that doesn't mean it's written in a way a simple cowboy can understand. When you find a Bible written for cowboys, I'll read it."

Those words stayed with me all day, and they're still with me to this day. That night I went home and started paraphrasing the New Testament in the words of a cowboy. I started with the Gospels—Matthew, Mark, Luke, and John. The Gospels ain't just words on a page. They guide us through the dusty trails of Jesus's life, His teachings, and His sacrifice. Each Gospel is a trailhead, invitin' us to ride closer to Jesus, see Him with fresh eyes, and follow His lead.

You'll find those words at the top of every devotion in this book. The Simplified Cowboy Version, or the SCV, is not a Bible. It's not a translation from the original language. It's just a study aid. My goal, prayer, and desire is that a cowboy would take the Simplified Cowboy Version, read it, and then wonder, *Is this really what the Bible says?* Then they would get a real Bible and read it.

That's the goal. That's my bull's-eye.

I hope you hit it.

THE GOSPELS—THE STORY OF JESUS IN FOUR PARTS

Let's dive into the heart of the Good Book, where we find not just one but four precious treasures known as the Gospels. Like four trails leading to the same windmill with Living Water, Matthew, Mark, Luke, and John paint a portrait of our Savior, each with their own colors and strokes.

Matthew, he's like a storyteller by the campfire, recountin' the lineage of the King born in a humble stable. He lays out the Message on the Mesa like a trail map, showin' us the way to live and how to ride for Him. With every word, he beckons us to follow Jesus.

Mark, well, he's like a cowboy who cuts straight to the chase. His Gospel is a whirlwind, a ride through the dusty tracks of miracles and teachings. He shows us a Savior who's always on the move, healin' the sick, feedin' the hungry, and tamin' storms with just one word. Mark reminds us that even in the whirlwind of life, Jesus is our anchor.

Luke, now there's a gentler trail, a journey through the fields and hills of compassion. He shines a light on the lost sheep, the prodigal son, and the Good Samaritan. His Gospel whispers of a Savior who came for all, who sought out the broken and the forgotten. Through Luke's eyes, we see a Jesus who mends hearts and welcomes everyone with arms wide open.

And then there's John, like an old cowboy sharin' tales by the firelight. His Gospel goes deep, unveilin' the mysteries of the Word made flesh. He describes the Light that shines in the darkness, the Vine that nourishes us, and the Cowboy who lays down His life for His sheep. John's Gospel takes us beyond the surface, invitin' us into the very heart of God's love.

The Gospels ain't just words on a page. They guide us through the dusty trails of Jesus's life, His teachings, and His sacrifice. Each Gospel is a trailhead, invitin' us to ride closer to Jesus, see Him with fresh eyes, and follow His lead.

In the following pages, we will be taking a close look at the books of Matthew, Mark, Luke, and John. As you read through each devotion, remember that you're not just readin' stories. You're ridin' the same paths of those who followed Jesus in the flesh. So, saddle up with these four cowboys, let their words shape your heart, and ride toward the source of our salvation.

Let's ride.

Finding Excitement in the Mundane

Before Jesus was born, Joseph had asked for Mary's hand in marriage. Joseph had been honorable toward Mary and she was unspoiled. But before they could get hitched, Mary became pregnant through the power of the Holy Ghost.

MATTHEW 1:18

Come on, admit it. The first Gospel book starts off with a boring genealogical list. Within the first seventeen verses, we're lost. Who are these people, and what does it really matter?

Well, while it may seem mundane or boring, there are many really cool things in the list. For example, there are five women in Jesus's genealogy, and you won't believe their stories!

Tamar was not a Jew. She was abandoned by her father-in-law, Judah, after being married to two of his sons and having no kids. She dresses up like a prostitute and gets pregnant by Judah, then blackmails him.

Rahab was a member of what is portrayed as a hostile indigenous population called the Canaanites, which was Israel's greatest enemy at the time. She was a prostitute who hid two Jewish spies during the fall of Jericho. She lied to protect them, and only her family was saved when Israel conquered the city.

Ruth was a member of a group called Moabites who were known for their worship of false gods and sexual immorality. After her husband and his family died, she left all she knew so she could stay with her Jewish mother-in-law, Naomi. Times were rough, but one of Naomi's relatives, Boaz, marries her. Oh, and her new mother-in-law is the prostitute Rahab.

Bathsheba was bathing on her roof when King David saw her from his palace. He "wanted" her; and what the king wants, the king gets. There were two problems, though. One, she got pregnant. Two, she was married to one of David's mighty men. David ordered that particular mighty man, Uriah, to the front lines of the war, so he died. David then married her, but because of his actions, their firstborn son died. Their next son was Solomon; he became king and the wealthiest and wisest man ever to walk the earth (besides Jesus, of course).

Mary was probably twelve to fourteen years old, but because of her faithfulness to God, He chose her to be the only virgin in history to give birth . . . to the Son of God—conceived not of man, but of the Spirit of God.

COWBOY CALL

God has a habit of using ordinary people in extraordinary ways. It doesn't matter if you're twelve or 112. It doesn't matter if you're educated or not. God can and wants to work through *you*. Get ready, and the time will come.

One Bad Hombre

After the strangers had lit out, an angel came to Joseph while he was dreamin'. "Saddle up," the angel told him. "Ride hard for Egypt and hunker down there until I tell you it's safe. Herod's gonna start killin' all the kids and he's hopin' Jesus is one of 'em."

MATTHEW 2:13

When Jesus was born, Herod was the king of Judea (often referred to as Herod the Great). This dude was one bad hombre. No one really liked him because he always sought Rome's favor. He was so disliked that he hired over two thousand soldiers as personal bodyguards to keep him safe.

There's a common misconception surrounding the Christmas story that the Magi (wise men) went straight to Jesus and the manger, but that isn't what actually happened. They went to Herod and asked where the new king was. This bothered Herod immensely because he really liked being king and didn't want to share his throne. He tricked the Magi into finding the baby King, saying he wanted to worship Him as well.

Truth? He really just wanted to find Jesus and kill Him.

An angel appeared to the wise men after they had found Jesus in Bethlehem and told them not to report back to Herod and reveal Jesus's location.

When Herod realized his plan had failed, he took matters into his own hands and had all the boys in the area who were two years old or younger killed. This is known in history as the Slaughter of the Innocents.

Then an angel appeared to Mary and Joseph telling them to flee to Egypt to protect baby Jesus. They remained there until Herod died.

Some historians claim that Herod knew he wasn't liked—so much so that he didn't want his death to be celebrated. So, this bad hombre planned to have many popular and influential people killed when he died to ensure that the nation would mourn his death. Fortunately, that wasn't carried out when he died because his son and Herod's sister supposedly kept it from happening.

COWBOY CALL

Authentic Christianity isn't for sissies. We were never promised an easy ride. You must learn to lean on God's strength . . . 'cause you're gonna need it.

John the Barbarian Baptist

"I dunk folks in water as a symbol that they want to change the way they think and live."

MATTHEW 3:11

Imagine your preacher coming in on Sunday morning, unwashed and unshaved while wearing a cowhide poncho cinched with a leather belt and nothing else. He immediately starts criticizing all the elders and deacons and every convention, denomination, and religious institution.

He doesn't stop with mere criticism of their ways. He calls them a den of rattlesnakes and tells them they are all going to burn in hell.

How barbaric!

At lunch, he doesn't go down to the café for steak and taters. He gets some grasshoppers and honey out of his lunch pail.

And then . . . you find out he is Jesus's cousin on Mary's side.

You would think Jesus would put a stop to his antics. On the contrary, Jesus said there was no one born who was greater than John the Barbarian Baptist.

John wasn't preaching three-piece suits and worship songs. He was preaching a life-changing transformation.

I think we've grown numb to the true meaning of "being saved" or "giving your life to Christ." Maybe it would be better understood as "swearing absolute and total allegiance to the Man and mission of Jesus Christ" . . . not just until Sunday service is over, but until your life is.

COWBOY CALL

Christianity isn't a Sunday thing. It's not a Wednesday-night thing either. It's not organs, pianos, and lead guitars. It's total transformation. It doesn't happen overnight, but it does happen. You cannot come face-to-face with the risen Savior and remain unchanged. If you're not all in, you're probably not in it at all.

From Bad News to the Good News

Jesus heard that His buddy John the Baptist had been thrown in jail so He rode back to Galilee.

MATTHEW 4:12

Jesus gets word that His buddy (John the Barbarian Baptist) has been thrown into prison, and He immediately goes and rescues him, right? Nope. He rides off to Galilee—the other direction.

John remains in prison, where his head is eventually chopped off! This doesn't seem right, does it? Jesus had just said there was no one greater than John the Barbarian Baptist. Jesus also said that he'd never leave us nor forsake us, right? This leaves many believers shaking their heads in confusion.

Listen, Jesus didn't forsake John. Sometimes bad things happen to great people. There is no greater prize in heaven than for those who have given their very lives riding for the Brand. Why would Jesus take that away from John?

I know, I know, I know. It doesn't seem right, but what if we understood things differently? Jesus also said that we should take up our cross and follow Him. I hope I don't have to remind you where the cross led to.

We all want an easy life. We want to be comfortable,

secure, safe, and healthy. Unfortunately, it just doesn't work that way. God uses pain and suffering to grow us and guide us. And the truth is, we were promised that we would have troubles. The good news? He will never leave us—He will love us and equip us through the ups and downs. He can even bring us joy and peace during our hardest seasons. So while we will face hard times, there will never be a moment when we are facing it all by ourselves.

COWBOY CALL

Authentic Christianity is anything but comfortable. Jesus came to save our souls, not our earthly lives. Are you willing to give your life for Christ, or is your faith dependent upon your current life circumstances?

The Message on the Mesa

"Y'all are the salt of the earth."

MATTHEW 5:13

In Matthew chapter 5, Jesus is teaching His disciples, but a whole bunch of other people gather around too. This teaching is called the Beatitudes.

Jesus teaches them all the benefits of being humble, of wanting to do right, of giving mercy to others, of being pure in our thinking, and the list goes on. I don't think there's a single one of us who can do all those things all the time. But maybe Jesus wasn't just describing what *we* should be doing. Maybe He was describing what *He* was doing.

Jesus knows we'll miss the target, but the Good News is that He came to do for us what we can't do for ourselves. Of course, it's good to strive for these things. But Jesus was giving us a trail to follow—one that He cleared for us.

My favorite part of the Beatitudes is very subtle. In verses 1–12, the same phrase is repeated: "Blessed are the ________." Fill in the blank with those things we spoke of earlier (humble, meek, merciful, etc.). Jesus uses this phrase to include *everyone*. But have you ever felt lost in the "everyone"? I think we all have. But in these verses, Jesus makes *an offer* to everyone.

Imagine you're at the Sermon on the Mount (or as I like to call it, the Message on the Mesa). Thousands of people are there to listen to Jesus—the greatest Preacher ever to live—so He knows how to work a crowd. There's something for everyone, and everybody's drinking in every word He says. Each word rings in their ears, reining in their hearts. Nobody has ever explained things like this. This is something new and special, and you know it.

And then it happens.

He turns and looks at you.

Instead of saying, "Blessed are the ________," He says, "Y'all [you] are the salt of the earth." And He's looking right at you when He says it.

Jesus is a personal God. You are not lost in the "everyone" He knows you and wants you to know Him.

COWBOY CALL

Try something this week. Take Jesus with you everywhere. Visualize that He is right beside you. Talk to Him about everything and everyone you come in contact with. Like a running dialogue in your head, talk to Him. Tell Him about your struggles. Tell Him about your favorite horse hay while you're at the feed store. Get to know Him, and you'll learn a lot about yourself.

Runnin' Off at the Mouth

"When you talk to the Boss, don't run your mouth off like an auctioneer who don't know when to say 'Sold!' Just repeatin' the same words over and over and over again don't get your prayers answered."

MATTHEW 6:7

In verses 7 through 13, we read the famous "Lord's Prayer." Many people learn it as a nighttime prayer as kids. But before Jesus shows us how to pray, He tells us how *not* to pray.

He tells us not to go runnin' off at the mouth. Using fancy words and repeating the same things over and over won't get you anywhere.

So, how does He tell us to pray?

Our Boss, who owns the heavenly pastures in the sky, may Your name be revered above all others (Matthew 6:9). Know who you're talking to. I mean, you *really* need to understand who you're talking to.

I hope Your pastures come soon, and I hope we all do what You want us to down here—just like things are done up there on Your spread (Matthew 6:10).

Our goal is, and always should be, oneness with God.

Jesus tells us to pray for what *God* wants.

Bring us today everything we'll need to get us by . . . (Matthew 6:11).

God wants to provide for us, His kids. Well, maybe He doesn't just want to provide; He wants you to know that *He* is the provision.

. . . and look the other way when we fail You. Help us also to look the other way when our partners fail us (Matthew 6:12).

Why should we forgive others? Listen, every single time you break God's law—or, in other words, every single sin—it is a slap on God's face, yet He forgives time and again. All the mean things ever done against you will never get close to the amount of meanness you've had against God.

And don't let us fall into gopher holes that will kill us, but keep us safe and sound from evil (Matthew 6:13).

If the only thing God ever, and I mean ever, did for you was forgive you of your sins, it would be all you need. If He never gave us wisdom or the gifts of His Spirit, we'd still have everything. But the fact that He does all these things in addition to forgiving us is really incomprehensible.

COWBOY CALL

Is it easy or hard for you to forgive? If you've been forgiven for *everything*, maybe it's time for you to forgive that one person for that one thing.

Being Judgy

"Don't make opinions about what others do, and no opinion will be made about you. The way you treat others is the way you will be treated. The judging eye you cast upon others will be the same judging eye that will be cast on you. Don't criticize your partner's horse for slinging its head when you can't even get on your own horse without gettin' bucked off. How can you offer to help your friend out with his horse when you can't even put a saddle on yours? That's just bein' a hypocrite! When you get your horse goin' good and steady, then you can offer to help your partner."

MATTHEW 7:1–5

I can't tell you how many times I've heard people say, "You can't judge me." There's a common misconception that Christians are not to judge, but that's not really the case. People who are opinionated would likely be deemed judgmental by many. But can we really go through life without having an opinion? I don't think we can. But I do think we can do something else.

We can have a good opinion of others. And if we're going to make an assumption, let's assume something good. This could even mean assuming that maybe someone's behavior at the moment is a result of a hardship that you know nothing about.

Jesus tell us not to judge harshly or incorrectly. If a friend is having an affair, it is not judging them to tell them that it is a sin. The Bible already declares that to be wrong. God has already judged this type of behavior as sinful.

I think a better way to understand what Jesus is saying is to think about it as nitpicking. No one likes a nitpicker. He's saying that since He isn't nitpicking everything you are doing, you have no business nitpicking others.

Grace and mercy flow from God so easily, maybe it's time we start being willing to give the same thing to others.

COWBOY CALL

Start trying to make good assumptions about others in the hardest circumstances. Make excuses for people. That should be easy. We make enough excuses for ourselves.

Quit Squallin'

Then Jesus jumped in the boat and they headed for the other side of the lake. All of a sudden, a boat-sinker of a storm blew in. But Jesus had His hat down over His eyes and slept through it. The disciples were frettin' and fearin' that this was gonna be the end of them all. They finally woke Jesus up by shakin' Him and saying, "Jesus, save us!! We're all gonna drown!" Jesus shook His head patiently and said, "Quit actin' like a bunch of sissies! You ain't got very much faith at all, do you?" Jesus got up, stretched, and told the wind to shut-up and the waves to sit down . . . and they did. The hands were shocked, stunned, and amazed and asked, "What kind of hombre is this? Even the wind and the waves listen at Him!"

MATTHEW 8:23-27

It's easy to read these stories and think that we would've had more faith than these sissies, but you wouldn't. We've all been scared—whether inside or outside—and we have a knack for squallin' our fool heads off at any storm in life.

We run to Jesus to "fill Him in" on what's happening. But Jesus is never surprised by anything. He's not going to "wake up," look around, and say, "Whoa! We better do something before something bad happens." No matter what, Jesus is *never* surprised, and He never freaks out.

I remember one time I was riding a colt and got bucked off. (Well, not really, because I never hit the ground.) I ended up on the horse's neck, where I held on for dear life. Yes, my arms and legs were wrapped around the horse's neck like a baby monkey holding on to his momma. Then my buddy got there. Ralph grabbed me by my belt and lifted me back in the saddle.

While I was squallin', Ralph was laughing! I thought the world was ending, and Ralph sounded like he'd never felt more alive!

Listen, I'm not saying Jesus is going to calm every storm in your life. There are times when you are going to be scared. Just remember, when the fear hits you, that God isn't surprised. He knew this was going to happen. He knows what the outcome will be. And He's riding right beside ya.

COWBOY CALL

What are some areas of your life where you wonder if God is really paying attention or if He's asleep on the bow? Does it feel like Jesus is asleep in the hammock when you need Him the most? Well, maybe that's a sign that you need to chill. So grab some iced tea and put your boots up for a while.

Gatherin' Mavericks

When Jesus left there, He saw a guy named Matthew sitting at the Tax Collector's shack. "Come on," He told him and Matthew left everything right there and went with Him. Jesus went to Matthew's house and supped with him. A lot of Matthew's friends, mostly outlaws and politicians that were crooked, came and ate with them and Jesus's hands. When the Religious-Know-It-Alls (Pharisees) seen this, they asked Jesus's cowboys, "Why does your trail boss eat with outlaws and no-accounts?" Jesus heard 'em and said, "The healthy cattle don't need a Vet, the sick ones do. You need to head off and ponder what this means: 'I want mercy, not sacrifice.' Because I haven't come to round up the gentle cattle, but I have come to gather the mavericks."

MATTHEW 9:9-13

Anyone who can sit on a horse without falling off can gather cattle.

All you do is take several people, get on the other side of the cattle, and push them toward the pen. But there always seems to be that one cow, or one calf (or both), that refuse to cooperate. They'll jump fences, and many times we end up roping them. That's something 99 percent of the world cannot do.

When first-time cowboys are asked how many cattle they gathered, they usually stick their chests out and say, "We gathered ninety-nine."

Then, when the old hands are asked the same question, they smile and say, "Just one."

Jesus is an old hand. Better yet, He's the Top Hand. He didn't come down here to trail-ride behind a bunch of compliant cattle. He came to rope and doctor the ornery ones that needed saving, not the ones headed to the gate already.

This devotional is for the ornery ones. It's for the ones who are brushed up, and most of the time, bad-hurt by something and someone. It's for you—the wild cowboys and cowgirls who are jumping fences or for those willing to work and care for the fence jumpers.

Either one you happen to be, I'm glad we found you.

COWBOY CALL

When's the last time you did something crazy for God? When was the last time you bucked the system and followed Jesus no matter the cost? How long will you wait before you do it again?

If you've been forgiven for everything, maybe it's time

for you to forgive
that one person
for that one thing.

A Loss for Words

"Watch your backs with men. They will hand you over to the local sheriffs and beat you within an inch of your life, right there in the churches. Because of Me, you will be taken before governors, presidents, and later, even to those who aren't Jews, so that you can tell them about who I am. Don't fret about what you're supposed to say when they arrest you though. When the time comes, I'll give you the words that you'll need. It won't be you that'll be talkin' at 'em, it'll be the Spirit of God speakin' through you."

MATTHEW 10:17-20

How many times have you wondered what to say in a situation? We plan, ponder, and wonder if we will have the right words. There are books, sermons, and podcasts galore about how to tell someone about Christ.

But Jesus tells us that this is all in vain. Sure, we should grow in our knowledge and hone our abilities, but when it comes time for the nut-cuttin', we don't have anything to fear. The Spirit of God, who lives in all believers, will do the talkin' for us. All you have to do is believe and then give Him the reins.

Go out in faith and don't be afraid to open your mouth a little or a lot (unless you're chewin' food). Trust that God is going to give you the words He wants you to speak. And don't be surprised if He asks you not to say anything . . . silence is oftentimes the most powerful. If it ain't from God, don't say it.

But that's not all, at all.

Have you ever wondered what would happen if someone said, "Deny Jesus, or I'll cut your head off!"? How would you respond—really? There's not a lot of things scarier than that.

Actually, if I'm honest, I'm a little scared of that situation. Because I know how I want to respond, but actually doing it is another matter entirely.

But this is where I find my peace: if God is willing to give us words, wouldn't He give us the courage we need to match them? Well, of course, He would! I think we sell God off so cheaply. In other words, we limit Him. He's going to give us everything we need. If you don't have it, you don't need it.

COWBOY CALL

What have you been fretting about? What is it in your life that is stealing your peace? Start believing that God has already given you all that you need, and if you do end up needing more, you can trust that God will provide it.

A Lick of Sense

"This right here's the truth: No woman has ever given birth to someone greater than John the Baptist. But the sorriest cowboy in God's Green Pastures [the Kingdom of Heaven] is greater than John. From the days of John the Baptist until right now, the Pastures of Heaven have been ridin' this way hard and many ruthless people have been attacking it. Until John came, all the world had been waitin' and talkin' and lookin' forward to this time right here. If you'll open your minds and hearts to understand this, he is just like the great cowboy Elijah, who wasn't scared to tell folks the truth and tell them about Me comin'. If you got a lick of sense you'll be able to understand what I'm tellin' you."

MATTHEW 11:11-15

Jesus says that no one is greater than John the Barbarian Baptist. But then He adds that even the sorriest cowboy who ever lived, who repented of his evil ways and saddled up for God, is greater than John.

And ironically, I think John would have agreed.

When I see a person who didn't grow up on the back of a horse or wasn't raised on a ranch learn how to rope and ride, I hold them in greater regard than one who's never known anything except cowboying.

John wasn't one to toot his own horn. He was more like a grizzled cow boss who knew his way 'round the ranch. He could rope and ride with the best of 'em, but his true grit shone when he led others to the waterin' hole of Jesus.

Now, picture this: a greenhorn, fresh off the wagon, learnin' to rope and ride. When a fella who never felt leather under his hands manages to rope something, that's a sight that earns respect. Same goes for those who find their way to God's side despite not growin' up in the church pews.

Here's the kicker: it don't matter if you ain't sung a hymn or quoted Scripture by heart. Your past don't define you, partner. It's the future that's ripe for the pickin'.

Remember, friend, you ain't just ridin' solo. Jesus—the greatest Top Hand of 'em all—He's leadin' the way. And if you heed His call, well, you'll find yourself ridin' a trail that's greater than any you've known before. So don't dawdle, don't look back—saddle up. What you're looking for is waitin' just over the hill.

COWBOY CALL

Don't let what you're not, tell you what you are. Stop making excuses for why you can't, and start realizing that you can and you should. Strive to learn something new and have the courage to be a beginner.

Making Rules Out of Rewards

Jesus rode through a wheat field on the day that God had told everyone to relax and rest. His cowboys were famished and picked some of the grain to eat. When the Religious-Know-It-Alls saw this, they said to Jesus, "Look at that! Your cowboys are breakin' God's law and workin' on the day He told us to rest." He answered, "Haven't you heard what David did when his crew was hungry? He entered God's church, and all of them ate the food that had been left there as offering to God. They weren't supposed to do that. Only the priests are supposed to eat that food. . . . I'm tellin' you that someone better than a church building is standin' right here. Religious hypocrites don't ever understand these words, 'I want a relationship, not a religion.' The Son of Man is Boss over the day of rest."

MATTHEW 12:1-4, 6-8

When God made everything, He worked for six days and then rested on the seventh. He set the model for work (six days), and His reward was a day of rest (the seventh day).

Instead of being happy about having a day off, the Jews started making rules out of the reward, forbidding certain actions on the Sabbath (day of rest). In fact, from sundown on Friday until sundown on Saturday (the Jewish Sabbath), you can't even push an elevator button because that is considered "work"!

That's what religion does. It takes the rewards of God and makes rules out of them to use against people. One of these examples is tithing. If I offered you $1,000 and asked if you'd give $100 back to me, would you take it? Of course, you would! You would do it all day long . . . and be happy about it.

Nowadays most people look at tithing as a punishment instead of a reward. God even said in Malachi that if we gave just a tenth of what He gave us in the first place, He would open up the floodgates of heaven and pour out a blessing on us that we couldn't even hold.

Religion tends to turn a "want to" into a "have to." I think this is really emphasized in the verse when Jesus said, "Someone better than a church building is standin' right here." Jesus isn't looking for how good you can follow rules but how deep your relationship with Him is.

COWBOY CALL

If you're ready for a deeper relationship with Jesus, make Him a part of your everyday life, not just Sunday. Ask for His guidance and listen for His leading. If you don't hear anything at first, it's okay. Listening is a skill that takes practice.

Storytellin'

His cowboys came up to Him and asked Jesus, "How come you just tell stories to people?" He nodded in understandin' and said, "You can understand these stories, but some cannot. These stories reveal the true nature of God's Green Pastures. Cowboys that are willin' to listen and try to understand the real meaning behind the stories will be trusted with secrets that others will not be. But those that won't listen, everything will be taken from 'em. I tell these cowboy stories because they see what I do, but they don't really see anything at all. They're lookin', but they don't see. They hear the stories, but they're not even listening. They understand, but they don't savvy. This is why the great cowboy Isaiah said, 'You hear, but you don't listen. You see, but you don't understand. The hearts of the cowboys have become calloused. Their ears don't hear and their eyes don't see. Therefore, they can't ride with Me and let Me fix what ails them.'"

MATTHEW 13:10-15

I love the stories Jesus told. The Christian word for these stories is "parables." That means a story with a message.

When I was first asked to preach, I had no idea what that even entailed. I didn't go to seminary or have any formal training apart from reading the Good Book every day. So, when it came time for me to prepare my first sermon, I went to the red letters in my Bible. The red letters mean it was Jesus talking. He told stories that people could relate to and understand.

Well, at least the ones who wanted to listen and learn.

So, that's what I did. I told stories with a message. Everyone loves a good cowboy story, especially one with a good message. I've built an entire ministry based off of stories—just like Jesus did.

But you have a story too. Every single minute of every single day, your story is unfolding. Your story fits into the larger story that is being written by God. Open your eyes as you live your story. Open your ears to what God is telling you. You've got a part to play in this story, and it's not a small one.

Someone's life might just start with your story. Start paying attention to it.

COWBOY CALL

If you ever have the opportunity to tell your story (or "give your testimony," as many churches would say), let me give you an easy-to-follow, three-part method. First, tell what your life was like before Christ, then how you came to truly follow Him, and finally, what your life is like now. Your story might change someone else's forever. Be ready.

Tying Things Together

So John's head was chopped off and brought on a tray to the daughter who then took it to her momma. John's crew then came and laid claim to his body and went and buried it on Boot Hill. Then they went and told Jesus what had happened. When Jesus heard the news, He rode off out into the pasture to be alone. But a bunch of people saw Him ride out and they followed Him. When Jesus got back from His ride, He felt sorry for all those that had gathered and waited on Him. He took pity on 'em and healed all that were ailing. When the sun was goin' down, Jesus's crew came up and told Him to send everyone back to town so they could get 'em some supper. But Jesus said that it weren't necessary. "Y'all feed 'em."

MATTHEW 14:10-15

Remember a few pages back, when we read that John the Barbarian Baptist had been thrown into prison? Well, he ended up losing his head over the deal. When Jesus found out, He rode out to be alone. That's what we all do in some way or another when we lose a loved one.

But during this time, one of the greatest miracles the world has ever seen took place. Instead of getting mad about all the people around while He was trying to mourn John's death, Jesus decided to make 'em supper!

This event is known as "The Feeding of the Five Thousand."

It's easy to separate these two events, but I think they are intrinsically tied together. One man had died, but probably fifteen thousand folks (they only counted the men in the five thousand, so you know there were at least one thousand more when you counted the women and children) were fixing to be given a chance to eat at the feet of the Son of God.

We may not always understand why things happen like they do, but we can rest in the hope that God is good and that He will never let a sacrifice go unused for the benefit of someone else.

And He allowed His Son to be the final sacrifice so that everyone who believes will benefit for eternity.

But did you notice what else Jesus did? He healed all who were ailing.

Jesus was having a rough day, and what did He do? He helped others. He didn't focus on Himself even when He wanted to be alone. That's a great cowboy right there.

COWBOY CALL

The next time you're having a rough day, use Jesus's example. First, go be by yourself and pray. Then, go help someone else. It's real easy to get caught up in the "poor, pitiful me" thoughts, but that's hard to do while praying and helping others.

Unfit for the Outfit

Pete asked Jesus, "What was You talkin' about when You said there are things that make a person unfit in the Boss' eyes?" Jesus told him, "Don't any of you have a clue what I was talkin' about? Don't you understand that anything you put in your mouth goes into your belly and will eventually find its way out of your body? But the words that come out of your mouth come from your heart. These words are what will make you unfit accordin' to the Boss. Out of your heart comes the awful things like: killing, cheatin' on your spouse, gross sexual excitement, horse thieving, goin' back on your word, and talkin' crap about other people. These are the things that the Boss don't like and these are the things that make you unfit."

MATTHEW 15:15-20

This is probably where some of you will run off. If you do, I'll let you go. I know what I'm fixing to say will rub some folks the wrong way, and I'm prepared for that.

Jesus said that it's not what goes into your mouth that can make you unfit for His outfit, but what comes out of it. Many folks have taken this to mean cussing. I don't think it does.

Cussing is actually slang for *cursing*. To curse someone means you're trying to inflict harm on them or passing judgment that's reserved for God. I think telling someone to "go to hell" is worse than any four-letter word. Maybe not from a moralistic standpoint, but certainly from a spiritual one.

I think cuss words do far less damage than all the gossip that is dressed up fancy as a prayer request. Talking behind someone's back damages our very souls! We're snide and pride ourselves on "calling it like it is." I think these things make us unfit for the outfit far more than using a four-letter word.

Now, I've been around cattle and cowboys a long time, and while they might cuss a cow under their breath, they wouldn't dare gossip about you or talk trash about their neighbor. They might go tell it to their face, but never the cowardly way of behind their back.

Once again, I'm not condoning filthy language, but there are far more unfit things that come out of Christians' mouths that no one bats an eye about . . . but we should.

COWBOY CALL

If the words we say reveal the true nature of our hearts, what does that say about us? Words have power, and we should use them wisely. That means not saying things we don't mean. Watch what you say . . . and how you say it.

Soul Swappin'

Then Jesus said to all the cowboys, "If y'all want to continue on in this crew, you need to forget about what you want and start focusin' on what the Boss wants. You gotta be willin' to give up your life and ride with Me. What will you get if you gain everything this world has to offer and you still lose your soul? What can a man swap that's worth his soul?"

MATTHEW 16:24-26

What is your soul worth? What is it that you would trade eternal rest and happiness for? I'll tell you what you'd swap it for. You'd swap it for football on Sunday. You'd swap it for a roping instead of a mission trip. You'd swap it for watching Netflix instead of reading Nehemiah. The lake seems a lot more attractive than listening to a sermon.

When you isolate these things, none of them are inherently evil or bad. But Jesus said that we had to give up *our lives*, and most of us can't give four Sundays in a row to God. We can spend $150,000 on a living-quartered horse trailer and new truck to pull it, but we don't consistently give God even the scraps of what we have left.

You see, when we swap a sermon for Sunday football once, it'll be easier to do again. So, we do it again. When we swap spreading God's Word for a roping, it's easier to do again. So, we do it again. You get the point.

I don't think going to church saves you. I don't think going on a mission trip is going to give you a golden ticket. But my point is that we must all really evaluate if we are giving God our lives or just some leftovers.

COWBOY CALL

My friend Willie started attending services at my church and nonprofit online discipleship and program, Save the Cowboy, about four years ago, and yesterday he preached his first sermon. Afterward, he said to me, "Stepping off that stage today and loving on everyone afterward was a dream come true that I didn't know I had. Thanks for believing in me." The reason I bring him up was because four years ago, the Spirit of God told me that in order to reach Willie, I had to give him a job. He's been the camera operator all these years, selflessly serving every single week. He even helped start a nonprofit that gets dads and kids together, and they serve in the community. He made God a priority in his life. No, he made God THE priority in his life. We should do the same.

Fed Up

Jesus said, "Good grief! Where is all of y'alls faith? How long am I gonna have to stick around and hold y'alls hand? I don't know how much more I can put up with. Bring that boy over here." Jesus looked at the boy and told the demon that was possessing him to get out. From that moment, the boy was fine. The cowboys asked Jesus, "How come we couldn't rope and drag that ol' demon out?" Jesus said, "'Cause you don't have a squirt of faith. With a bit of faith, you could move mountains; anything is possible."

MATTHEW 17:17-20

Prayers aren't just words you throw out hoping they will be heard. A prayer should be believed before it is ever uttered. We have vast promises and power available that we throw out like a kid in a candy store. "I want this . . . I want that . . . bless me, Lord, I pray."

But did you know there is something that you don't need to pray about?

I know, that sounds strange, especially when the Bible says to pray about everything. But what you don't have to pray about is whether you should do what God told you to do. You might have to pray for strength not to worry, but you don't have to pray whether you should or not. What you don't have to pray about is whether you should obey God when it is crystal clear what He expects from you. Instead of praying about whether to follow His guidance, you need to start praying for the strength, wisdom, and courage to ride the trail He has laid before you. Sometimes you just have to trust that His plans are always for your good and His glory.

Jesus told us that with just a squirt of faith, anything is possible. He didn't say that faith would guarantee a specific result. He said it was possible, not guaranteed. It's not about controlling outcomes, but about surrendering to God's perfect will. Trust me, He is answering your prayers—but it may not be today, and it may not be in the way you want it answered. You just have to have faith that He's got you and He wants the best for you, and then let it go.

COWBOY CALL

Try praying right now and throw all your faith into it, not for a particular outcome, but so that God might be glorified. Who knows? It's possible you'll get exactly what you ask for.

How to Handle Squabbles

"If a cowboy that works for Me does something to you that is against one of My rules (not yours), be a man and go talk to him about it. Let it be just between the two of you. Don't go round up all your buddies or even tell them what you're doin'. If he listens to you, y'all will be able to ride together. If he won't listen to you, go ahead and take another cowboy along so that neither side will be able to accuse the other of something that was said. If he still refuses to listen, take it to the men leadin' your crew. If he even refuses to listen to the cowboys I have chosen to be in charge of My outfit, just run him off. Treat him like you would a trespasser and get him off My place."

MATTHEW 18:15-19

Besides the command to love the Lord with all your heart and soul and love your neighbor as yourself, I think this is the most applicable and most needed command in the Bible.

It's saying that if you have a problem with someone, be a man and go talk to him face-to-face. If that don't work out, take someone else who hasn't been filled in on what's going on and try to work it out again. If it still doesn't work, then let them go.

The word *pandemic* is thrown around a lot. But a true pandemic has been going on for a long time, and that is cowardice. It's a lot easier to talk about someone behind their back. Throwing threats and gossip around is easier than doing what God says.

This passage isn't about proving who is right and who is wrong. The goal of this is reconciliation. The goal is to let light shine in the darkness that has come between two of God's kids.

COWBOY CALL

Now, who do you need to go talk to? Either go talk to them or let it go. Those are your only two choices.

“Those who
pat themselves
on their back
will end up
flat on their back.
And those

who cry out to God
with their face
down in sorrow
will be lifted
up to heaven."

LUKE 18:14

Bulls Giving Birth to Coyotes

A fellow walked up to Jesus and said, "Hey, amigo! What kind of good deeds do I have to do to get an eternal job on the Boss' place?"

"Why are you askin' Me about good things?" Jesus replied. "There is only One that fits the word 'good.' If you want an eternal place on the ranch, you must hold to all the commandments. . . . Don't kill, don't fool around on your spouse, don't rob, don't lie about other folks, respect your ma and pa, and take care of your neighbors better'n you take care of yourself."

"I've done all of these," the rich fellow said. "Is there anything else?"

Jesus smiled and said, "If you want to get an eternal spot on the ranch, go and give everything you got to those that don't have anything. By givin' everything you have away here, you will receive much more in heaven. Then, when you're done, come and ride with Me."

When the rich fellow heard this, he hung his head and walked away, unwillin' to do as Jesus asked.

MATTHEW 19:16-18, 19-22

Do you want to know what I am most asked to preach about by authentic cowboys who ride for God? It's not on how to be more blessed. It's not how to have a closer relationship with God. It's not even about how to know you are saved.

They always ask why I don't preach about tithing.

Tithing is the deal breaker for a lot of people. I've even been told that tithing is Old Testament and we aren't commanded to do that under the New Covenant. I just smile and say, "I don't disagree."

Yes, as we've mentioned before, one of the biggest rewards God offers is for tithing, but that was in the Old Testament (Malachi). God offered us untold blessings for just giving back 10 percent of what He gives to us. But I won't disagree; that is Old Testament.

That's when I point them to the New Testament, the one they claim to be under. God said in the Old Testament to give 10 percent. Jesus said in the New Testament, "If you want to get an eternal spot on the ranch, go and give everything you got to those that don't have anything."

COWBOY CALL

Why stop at the 10 percent God asked for? Go ahead and give everything like Jesus said. No? Maybe that's why Jesus also said in the same passage, *It's tough for a rich man to get an eternal spot on the ranch. It's probably easier for a bull to give birth to a coyote than a rich man to enter the Forever Pastures* (Matthew 19:23–24).

Grace in $100 Bills

"The cowboys who had been playin' cards at the saloon and drinkin' whiskey all day walked over and the rancher paid them one hundred dollars. When the cowboys who had been there since the sun came up walked over to get their wages, they assumed they would get much more, but they, too, were given one hundred dollars. When they saw that they had received the same amount for workin' all day as the last cowboys got for workin' an hour, they began to grumble and cuss about the rancher. 'These cowboys came up and only worked for an hour and barely broke one bead of sweat. You've paid them the same amount as us who've worked all day long in the heat, the sun, and the dirt!' But the rancher said to one of them, 'Cowboy, I ain't cheatin' you out of anything. You agreed to work for me today for one hundred dollars, and that's what I paid you. Take your wages and ride on out of here. I want to give every single cowboy that worked for me today one hundred dollars, regardless of how long they worked.'"

MATTHEW 20:9–14

I sat with a very sick man. I didn't know him well, but his wife was a staunch believer and one of the most giving people I'd ever met. He'd told her, "I'm not going to be one of those cowards that goes crying to God at the end. God knows my heart." Neither of us knew what he meant by that. I had one arm around his wife while my other hand was on his wrist. I felt his last heartbeat on earth. And then I couldn't stop crying because I didn't know what he meant and I didn't know where he stood with God.

Matthew 20:9–14 tells us that it's never too late. You can be the most dedicated Christian, living your life for Jesus 24/7, and get rewarded; or, on the flip side, you can end up accepting Him later in life after spending the majority of your time in disregard to God and His ways, and still get rewarded.

All you have to do is ask. Don't let pride stand in your way. I don't care if you've worked all day or just an hour, accept God's unlimited generosity today!

COWBOY CALL

Saying you've sinned too much to be saved is like saying you're too dirty to take a shower. Don't wait. Ask for forgiveness. Be cleansed.

A Different Jesus

Jesus walked into the church building and started running everyone out that was buying and selling things. He knocked over the money changers' tables and the chairs of those that were selling doves for sacrifices. "It was written long ago," Jesus said, "'My house will be a place where you could talk to Me,' but you have made it a den of thieves."

MATTHEW 21:12-13

Matthew 21 shows us a very different kind of Jesus than we're used to. He's not healing folks or bringing them back from the dead. He's not curing leprosy or driving out demons... well, maybe He was doing that last one a little bit.

Why is He knocking over tables and chairs?

The Temple had its own currency system. It was much like going to another country and trading your dollars for pesos. Why did they need to exchange money?

Because the sacrificial system was supposed to involve bringing the best-you-had-to-offer sacrifices. You were to bring a spotless lamb you owned or a white dove. The sacrificial system went from bringing the best you had to *buying* a sacrifice. And, of course, the Temple's doves that were for sale were better than yours.

So, people were allowed to come in and buy their sacrifices, but they had to use Temple currency. The money exchangers were basically giving dimes for dollars. I'm sure the exchange rate was far from fair.

Jesus was mad that His Father's house had turned into a moneymaking venture.

Religion is big business, and Jesus hated religion. He hated it so much that He went and turned it all over—literally.

Money is a sensitive topic today, just like it was back then. The Bible says that the *love of money* is the root of all evil, and no one is exempt—the church or the individual.

COWBOY CALL

Do you give God the best of what you have to offer? At my nonprofit, Save the Cowboy, we raise beef on our ranch and then give that beef away one package at a time to hungry families. The stuff we butcher is the best cattle we raise. They are the top of the line. We don't sell the best and give God what's left. We give God the best and then sell the rest. How can you do that in your life?

Not Caring What People Think

Then the Religious-Know-It-Alls tried to trap Jesus with His own words so they could arrest Him. They sent some people to ask Him, "We know You're a great cowboy and a good teacher of what the Boss wants. You don't care what men think about You or what they say. Since You don't care, is it right for us to pay taxes to Caesar?" Jesus knew they were tryin' to trap Him with their words, and He said, "Why are you dealin' words off the bottom of the deck and tryin' to trap Me with the dead man's hand of aces and eights? Show Me a dollar that you would pay your taxes with." They showed him a silver dollar, and He asked, "Whose picture is stamped on this dollar?" "That's Caesar's picture," they said. Then He told 'em, "If it has his picture on it, then give it back to him. Give to Caesar what belongs to Caesar and give to the Boss what belongs to the Boss." They didn't know what to say to this so they just left.

MATTHEW 22:15-22

The Pharisees and other religious people were constantly trying to trap Jesus with something they could hang Him over. They were right: Jesus didn't care what men thought, but He wasn't just out there running His mouth off either. Jesus was God in human flesh and had the wisdom of God to go with it.

Jesus was always pointing the way to God. He reaffirmed what our priorities should be: Give to God what is God's and give to man what is man's.

But let's not miss the real thing that's going on here. They're trying to trap Jesus. That's what this world does. It tries to trap the good. It's going to happen to you too.

The problem is that you don't see the trap until it closes. That's why it's called a trap. The only way to avoid it is to follow Jesus like He's leading you through a minefield. If He told you to step where He steps or you'd get blown up, then you'd probably do it.

That's what the Bible is for us. It's our path through the traps. It takes diligence and intentionality to pay attention to what's really important and not get caught up in the catcalls that distract us from the traps.

COWBOY CALL

Don't get caught up in the trap of meaningless conversations. You want to know how to spot a meaningless conversation? It looks exactly like a tumbleweed rolling aimlessly across the prairie, stirred by the wind but going nowhere. If it feels like someone is trying to prove you wrong, or make a point out of you, stop and ask God for the words to help you respond. He can give purpose to the conversation.

Elitism and Other Religious Nonsense

Jesus turned and talked to His cowboys and the rest of the folks that were sittin' around. He said, "The Hypocritical Preachers and the Lawyers of the Code are experts in the Law of Moses. Y'all need to do what they say, but don't act like they act. They sure as heck don't practice what they preach. They will load y'all down with impossible tasks that they wouldn't be willing to bear. They have silver on their saddles and jingle bobs on their spurs, just so y'all will think they are important. They are all talk and no action. They like the box seats at the rodeo and want to be the first in line at the chuckwagon. They care about bein' recognized at the feed store and bein' called by fancy titles. But y'all cowboys that ride for Me don't need fancy titles. . . . The one that is the top hand among you will be your servant that works like a pack mule. Whoever tries to rise above others will be thrown down and whoever lowers himself will be raised up."

MATTHEW 23:1-8, 11-12

I was sitting in a Waffle House one early morning waiting on an appointment. I was hungry, so I ordered some waffles. A man walked in, and all the staff greeted him as "Apostle."

I turned around expecting to see Peter, James, or John. What I saw wasn't any of them, but he sure seemed nice, and everyone seemed to love him.

He left his business card on the table next to me, and I stole a peek at it. Sure enough, it had "Apostle" in his name. Now, I'm not doubting his faith. He seemed like a really cool guy, but I'm not sure I would have gone around calling myself "apostle," and I'm pretty sure that's not what the Bible teaches.

Honestly, I don't even like being called "pastor." That's other people's way of describing me, but I have honestly just introduced myself as Kevin to everyone I meet. I don't like fancy titles. I'm just a guy riding for Jesus and doing what God called me to do.

What about you? It's so easy to get roped into the rhythm of it all. Think about it—do you feel like your calling is more important to the Kingdom of God than those around you? Do you have a fancy title you like to throw around to get special treatment? If so, maybe it's time to ask God if you're truly walking the path He's laid out for you or if you've strayed into the thorny brush of pride and self-importance. Ask Him to help you humble yourself, and follow His trail with a servant's heart, leaving titles and recognition behind in the dust.

COWBOY CALL

I wonder what would happen if we all loved the title that God gave us. He called us, "My children."

The Key to the End Times

"Two cowboys will be gatherin' cattle and one will be taken and the other left right there in the saddle. Two cowgirls will be feedin' horses and one will be taken and the other left standin' right there. Be on the lookout and don't get lax in the saddle. Keep both feet in your stirrups and one eye on the sky. You won't know when I'm comin' back, so be ready. You got to keep a sharp watch. If you knew what time a horse thief was comin', you would be ready with your rifle. Mark My words and be ready for the Son to come ridin' back down."

MATTHEW 24:40-44

I had a woman in a Walmart that was peddlin' their credit card one day ask me if I wanted to apply for one. I told her that I didn't have any credit cards and didn't want one. If I didn't have the money to pay for it, I didn't need it.

Fast-forward, and she found out that I was a preacher. Her eyes got wide, and she started in on all this end-times prophecy stuff. Quite frankly, I didn't understand a word she was saying. When she finally came up for air, she asked me, "So, when do you think the end will come, and who do you think the Antichrist is?"

I took a deep breath and said, "The most important thing to remember about the end times can be summed up in two little words."

Then I was silent.

I knew she wanted some time frame or a wild, outlandish conspiracy theory providing the day on which Jesus would come riding back over the hill to save us all. But when I didn't say anything more, she was about to pee her pants. She finally got tired of waiting and asked, "Well, what is it?"

I'd finally finished paying for all my stuff, and she had stayed right in line with me. I took another deep breath and finally said as I was walking away, "The most important thing to remember about the end times can be summed up in two little words: *Be ready.*"

COWBOY CALL

What does it mean to be ready? I used to think it was about being saved, and that is true. But what if one element of being ready means that you're looking forward to it? If you're ready to go on vacation, that doesn't just mean you're prepared to take the time off. It means you long for it and can't wait for the moment to arrive. You count down the minutes and hours. Think about that, and then ask yourself, *Am I ready?*

Cowboys and Sheepherders

"Then the Lord will turn to the goats on His left and say, 'Get these sorry mongrels off My spread! Put them on the killer trucks and ship them off to the fire that never goes out—the fire that was prepared for the devil and his demons! I was hungry and you refused Me food. I was thirsty and you laughed. I was a stranger in need and you ignored Me. Thorns cut My legs and it made no difference to you. I was sick and in jail and you never visited Me.' Then they will cry out, 'Lord, we never saw You hungry, thirsty, or any of those other things. If we would have seen You, we would have done something.' And He will answer, 'Listen to Me close. When you refused these things to the cowboys and cowgirls that rode for My Father's brand, you refused them to Me!' And then they will be shipped off to the fires of hell, but those cowboys and cowgirls that rode for the Father's brand will be turned out to lush, eternal pasture."

MATTHEW 25:41-46

I've always said that anyone can gather cows. But it takes someone special to gather sheep. In other words, any sheepherder can gather cows, but not every cowboy can gather sheep.

Sheep are harder to gather. To put it bluntly, they're stupid. They need special care in being protected, fed, doctored, and everything else you can think of. They don't stay together. They fight with each other. They run off in any direction that they're pointing. They even run right toward danger instead of toward the very ones who are trying to keep them safe.

Does that sound familiar at all?

It should, because it sounds just like you and me. Why? Because we are both the sheep and the shepherds. Too many times, we do the same things that make sheep hard to work with, but other times we have to step up and be the shepherd who deals with stupid creatures like ourselves.

Thankfully, Jesus knows we can't take care of ourselves. He wants to take care of us and steer us out of trouble. Other times, He uses us to help and take care of others who are headed the wrong direction.

COWBOY CALL

Do you let God take care of you, or are you self-reliant? I think we all have a self-reliant streak a mile wide inside us, but God wants us to lean on Him and have faith that He will take care of us. In which areas do you need to be less self-reliant?

Shuckin' Out on Jesus

As they rode over to Olive Hill, Jesus told them, "Tonight, all of y'all are gonna shuck out on Me. The Good Book says, 'The Boss will slay the Trail Guide and the herd will scatter.' But after I come back from the grave, I will meet ya'll in Galilee."

Pete said, "I don't care if everyone shucks out for the hills, I ain't leavin' You."

"I'm tellin' you the truth, Pete," Jesus said. "Before the sun comes up, you will deny that you ever rode with Me three times."

Pete stood up and stomped his foot as he said, "Even if I have to die with You to prove it, I will never deny ridin' with You." And all of Jesus's crew made the same vow and waved their hats in the air.

MATTHEW 26:31-35

We can make a bold statement by stomping our feet and insisting that we would never do this or that, but when the rubber hits the road, can we still stand firm in our convictions, or will we be swayed by our fears and doubts?

Peter denied Jesus because he was afraid, not because he had completely lost his faith. And we see this in John 21:7, when after Jesus's resurrection, Peter recognizes Him on the shore while fishing, then jumps into the water to get to Him. Maybe it was to make amends or offer an apology, or maybe he knew the only place for him was right next to his Savior.

In moments of doubt or fear, it's easy for us to distance ourselves from our faith, just as Peter did when he denied Jesus. But the beauty of Peter's story lies in his immediate recognition of the Lord and his eagerness to be close to Him once again. Like Peter, we, too, may have made promises to Jesus that we haven't kept, or we might have moments of weakness when fear overcomes our faith. Yet, just as Jesus forgave Peter and restored their relationship, He offers us the same forgiveness and grace. The lesson here is that even in our lowest moments, Jesus is waiting for us with open arms, ready to restore our faith and draw us close to Him.

COWBOY CALL

I pray that the next time you're put in a situation
to be who Jesus said you could be,
you will follow Him . . .
and that trail always leads to the foot of the cross.

Keep Yer Mouth Shut

When He was accused by the head honchos of the church, He didn't answer. Then Pilate asked Him, "Don't You hear what they are sayin' about You?" But Jesus didn't answer. He didn't say one word about any of the charges. His silence baffled Pilate.

MATTHEW 27:12-14

Jesus remained silent throughout His trials. Why? Some say He didn't want to be set free because He knew He had to endure the punishment in order to fulfill His mission. And that may be the case, but one thing I know for sure is that Jesus's ultimate battle wasn't with Pilate or the head honchos who were accusing Him—it was with the enemy of our souls.

Have you ever stopped to think about who you are arguing with? Is it really the person in front of you—you know, the one who insulted you or falsely accused you? Or is your ultimate battle with the enemy, who is, no doubt, the one who is really causing struggles and havoc and working to bring chaos to your life by any means possible? When you look at the bigger picture (and not what you see right in front of you), it changes the way you respond to the situation.

Our job is to listen to God and obey. Next time you find yourself in this situation, pray and ask God whether you should remain silent or if you should defend yourself, and if He leads you to speak, ask Him for the words to help you respond correctly. Rest assured, if He is involved in your response, you're riding down the right trail.

COWBOY CALL

Do you find it harder to remain silent or to speak up? Try stepping out of your comfort zone the next time something comes up. There's a time and place for both. Asking God for wisdom is the key.

Without
obedience to
the Word of God,
our ride
is on a stick horse,
waving our hats
in the air

and yelling, “Yeehaw” on Sunday mornings without doing anything.

Jesus: Liar or Messiah?

The winged rider said, "Y'all, don't be scared. I know that y'all are lookin' for Jesus, who was strung up and killed on that cross. But He ain't here! He has rode back from the dead just like He said He would. Y'all come take a look and see that I ain't pullin' your leg. Once yer satisfied that He ain't here, run and tell His cowboys: 'He has rode back from the dead and has struck a long trot for Galilee. There is where you'll meet Him.' I've said what I came to say."

MATTHEW 28:5-7

Can you imagine? Mary Magdalene, and Mary, the mother of James—them women come to that place where the Savior's body was laid. But it's empty—emptier than a water hole in a drought. A tomb, once a dwelling of darkness, now a canvas painted with the dawn of hope, greeted by angels' voices like wind rustling through the canyons.

What a moment, eh? Can you picture them women as they realize the weight of what they've witnessed? The promise, whispered by the One who walked on water and calmed the storm, had become a reality before their very eyes. It was a reality more vibrant, more life-changing, and more profound than anything that had ever happened in the course of human history. The resurrection of Jesus Christ was not just a historical event; it was the moment that changed everything. The empty tomb was the catalyst that transformed the fearful and discouraged disciples into bold proclaimers of the Gospel. It's about takin' those tidings and sharin' 'em like a cowboy sharin' tales of far-off lands and wild cattle. And just like them women, we're called to spread the word, to share the Good News that the Savior has risen and He offers new life.

So, next time the sun creeps over the horizon, remember that mornin' in that land of old, where angels proclaimed good news and an empty tomb sang a tale of renewal and redemption. It's a tale that echoes in our hearts today, remindin' us that promises made by the One who tamed the waves and set the stars in the heavens—well, them promises, they're meant to be trusted and shared, like a cherished yarn spun 'round a campfire.

COWBOY CALL

I love the sense of urgency the angels had. "Run and tell His cowboys!" they said. Does your faith have a sense of urgency to it? What would you do if you only had one day left on earth? And maybe we should be askin' ourselves why we aren't living like there's one day left . . . because one day, that will be true.

Who Is Mark?

This ain't about nothing except the good news of a man named Jesus, the Son of God. I reckon it all started when one of God's top hands, a fella named Isaiah, wrote this, "God said, 'I got a cowboy coming that is going to show you a new message and a new way of riding for Me. He's already shouting from the desert and tellin' y'all to get ready to saddle up for the Lord and ride right straight for Him.'"

MARK 1:1-3

We know him better as John Mark. While not one of the original twelve cowboys who rode with Jesus, he accompanied Paul on many missionary journeys.

Mark is probably the first account of Jesus ever written. He doesn't include the birth of Jesus, but he starts right where Jesus's ministry starts. He walked with giants of faith and rubbed shoulders with none other than the apostle Peter himself. Picture it: two fellas, sittin' under a starlit sky, sharin' stories like kinfolk gathered 'round the fire. John Mark, he soaked up Peter's tales of the One who turned water into wine and fed a multitude with a handful of loaves and fishes.

But John Mark was no shepherd or farmer. As he jotted down Peter's words, he became a storyteller of divine proportions, leavin' a legacy that'd stretch from one end of the earth to the other.

Mark had a way with words. Like a rope pullin' us closer to the heart of the Man who walked on water and healed the sick, he captures the moments that matter—that make you feel like you're sittin' a good horse in new country.

Mark's Gospel is like a river that winds through the soul, refreshin' and nourishin' as it goes. He tells it like it was—no frills, no fuss—just plain and simple truth.

For not being one of the twelve disciples, Mark plays a huge role in how we see Jesus today. Do you ever feel like you're not included? Like you aren't one of the important ones? If so, the Gospel of Mark proves that ordinary people, like you and me, can have a profound impact on other people's lives. We never know the ripple effects our faith can have on others.

COWBOY CALL

Next time you are feeling insignificant, think about what gifts God has given you and how you can use them where you are at this very time and place. God made you to live during this generation for a reason. It's time to believe it!

It Takes One to Know One

Jesus rode out again along the area close by the sea. A whole crowd came with Him, and He gave them a clinic on how to ride for God's outfit. As they continued on their travels to spread the good news, He saw a fellow named Levi sitting in a tax collector's booth. "Saddle up, cowboy," He said to him. Levi left everything right there and rode off with them.

MARK 2:13-14

A man I went to high school with ended up being a police officer. It shocked everyone because he was a thorn in the side of the police growing up. He never committed any serious crime, but even if he knew his fun was going to get him into trouble, he'd do it anyway.

But he had a change of heart and decided to help others so they didn't take the wrong path he'd taken. Some people called him a hypocrite, but I called him brave. It takes guts to admit you were wrong.

Jesus chose many of His disciples for the same reason. None of the twelve cowboys who rode with Jesus were religious leaders; they were rough men. Seven of them were fishermen, one was a tax collector, and the rest of their occupations are only speculation even though some of them had titles like "zealot."

You don't have to be perfect to follow Jesus. Just like He called those twelve rough cowboys who rode with Him, He calls people from all walks of life, with all their imperfections and flaws. He sees the potential in each one of us and believes in our capacity for change and growth.

No matter what you've done in your life—whether you've hurt the ones you love, drank too much, or stolen things—He is asking you to follow Him. And if you do, He can transform you into a faithful disciple with a new life and a real purpose. So, let us ride alongside Jesus with the same determination that those twelve cowboys had. He will give you the strength to become a better version of yourself, one step at a time.

COWBOY CALL

In Mark 2:13–14, Jesus called Levi to join His posse. There's some mighty fine guidance tucked away in them verses, so let's dig in:
Step one is to hear the call. Just like Levi, we gotta be willin' to lift our ears and listen when Jesus beckons.
Step two, don't be shy 'bout your past. Levi was a tax collector, but Jesus didn't judge him by his past.
Step three, embrace the change. Levi got up, left it all behind, and followed Jesus.
Step four, invite Jesus to the table. Levi threw a big ol' feast for Jesus. Let's remember to make Him the centerpiece of our gatherings and decisions.

THE "UNFORGIVABLE SIN"

"I'm telling you straight, every wrong can be forgiven, but anyone who rejects the love of God and attributes the Holy Spirit's work to the devil, that person's sin will not be forgiven." He said all this because they were accusing Him of being possessed by a demon.

MARK 3:28-30

What was Jesus talking about when He said there was a sin that could not be forgiven? In a nutshell, forgiveness is based on belief in Jesus and His sacrifice. If a person doesn't believe, then He cannot be forgiven.

What's harder to understand is that this isn't an intellectual belief. It is a life-altering belief. Someone who says they believe in Jesus without having a life-changing paradigm shift in the way they act and speak might want to reevaluate what they really believe. When you truly accept God's love, you are different than you were before. A weight lifted off your shoulders because you are no longer on your own. Not only are you able to lean on His strength and wisdom to take care of all your problems, but because you are given His peace and joy, you want to pass it along.

You can't help but share the kindness He shows to you with others. And this is life-changing.

Kinda makes you wonder why anyone would reject Him, doesn't it?

COWBOY CALL

God wants to forgive you. He wants to equip you with everything you need. He knows we're bound to get thrown or just fall off, but what matters is how we get back up. Be careful not to be hard-hearted. Jesus is sayin' all you have to do is have a heart that's open to change. Let that openness lead you to Him.

More and More

Then He added, "Don't let what I'm saying go in one ear and out the other. The closer you listen the more you'll start getting—and when you start getting it, you'll be given even more. Those who listen and apply what I say to do, they'll start catching on even more and more. But if you ignore the things I say, you'll end up losing more than you started with."

MARK 4:24-25

I often hear people say that they don't understand the Bible. It's one of the main reasons I started writing the Simplified Cowboy Version paraphrase, which you'll find at the top of every devotion in this book. It's just my way of sharing the Word with my kind, hardworking cowboys and cowgals. My hope is that they will read something that draws their interest, and then they'll go to a real Bible and see if it says the same thing.

When you start getting into the Word, you'll start seeing the bigger picture. You'll start seeing God in and through everything. You'll see Him in the vast, open skies that stretch on for miles, painting the most beautiful sunsets. You'll see Him in the rugged terrain, reminding you of His steadfastness amidst life's challenges. As you delve deeper into His Word, you'll see Him in the faces of the people you meet, recognizing His love and grace reflected in each of them.

Just like a seasoned cowboy reads the signs of the land and the sky, you'll become attuned to the signs of God's presence in your daily life. His wisdom will guide you like a trusty compass, and His love will be your lasso, drawing you closer to Him and to the path He has set for you.

COWBOY CALL

Listen close. Jesus ain't just talkin' 'bout hearin' with your ears; He's talkin' 'bout tappin' in to the truths that come from Him and doin' them. Tune in, lean in, and catch those whispers of wisdom. Share the bounty. As you gather the wisdom, the kindness, and the more, don't go hoardin' it. Spread it 'round, and let it shine like stars in a clear night sky.

Throwing Rocks at Jesus

Now the people that had been taking care of that herd of pigs ran off to tell everyone what had happened. People came running and the first thing they saw was Jesus sitting there talking to the man who had been possessed, but this time he was in his right mind. Word spread quickly about what happened and the people were afraid. They begged Jesus to leave the area.

MARK 5:14-17

The story about Legion is a famous one in the Good Book. Jesus cures a man who's possessed by a herd of demons. Jesus sends the demons into a herd of pigs, and they run off a cliff and die.

The possessed man had been terrorizing the community, and when the townsfolk went to see what had happened, Jesus was sitting there talking to the man like nothing had ever happened. He wasn't the same man as they knew before.

After such an astonishing miracle, why did the townsfolk throw rocks at Jesus like He was a cur dog preying on chickens? Exactly what had He done wrong in setting that poor man free?

Maybe they were afraid of such an amazing miracle because they'd never seen anything like it before. But they also could have been afraid that Jesus would cost them more than He already had. They depended on those pigs for food and income, and now they were down more than a few.

We're often willing to follow Jesus until it really costs us something. Jesus said following Him wouldn't cost us anything. He said it would cost us *everything* . . . and *everything* would be what we got in return.

Are you throwing rocks at Jesus because He allowed something or someone you depended on to be taken away? Maybe it's time to remember what He has given you. Look around, cowboy. See the sunrise over the rolling hills? Feel the warmth of the campfire on a cold night? Hear the soothing sound of a bubbling stream after a long day's ride? These are His gifts, signs of His presence, and reminders of His love.

So, put down those rocks and pick up gratitude. Embrace what He has given you, and trust that He knows the path you need to walk. When you do, you'll find that the journey becomes a whole lot easier, and the horizon holds even more promise than you ever imagined.

COWBOY CALL

Want to know what happened to the freed man? Well, he begged to go with Jesus, but Jesus said he couldn't come with Him. Instead, He told the man to go and tell others about Him and all that God had done for him. You see, the message never changes. Jesus fixes us, and then He wants us to tell others about the fixing. Are you quick to share what Jesus has done in your life, or do you struggle to even see Him in it?

Shunned at Home

After all those great things were done, Jesus struck a long trot back to His hometown, and His cowboys followed Him. When the day of rest came, Jesus went and did a little preaching at the local church. People who listened were wondering where He came up with all these different interpretations of God's Word. They also wondered where all His wisdom came from and if the miracles He had been performing came from the same place. They all shook their heads and kept asking one another, "Isn't this that carpenter? Isn't this Mary's son? Aren't those His sisters that live near here?" Because of all their questions, they didn't hear Him; because of their looking for answers elsewhere they couldn't see Him; and they got offended that this ordinary fellow would stand up in front and dare to teach them.

MARK 6:1-3

Ain't it somethin' how folks tend to hitch their horses to our past like a worn-out saddle? Same goes for Jesus. 'Fore He started turnin' water into wine and raisin' the dead, He was just a carpenter, workin' away like any regular Joe. But then, He's slingin' miracles left and right and spillin' wisdom that hit like a lightning bolt. They couldn't see that He was God and man.

You ever been there? Folks got a picture of who you were, now strugglin' to see the new trail you've carved for yourself.

But don't go losin' sleep over it. It's a road Jesus blazed Himself. Remember when He said, "If they dished out trouble to Me, reckon they'll serve you a slice too"? When you ride alongside the Savior, you're bound to feel the jolt of the good and the rough. Just like He didn't dodge the storms, we don't get to pick and choose our weather either.

When them echoes of yesteryears come a-knockin', ask yourself: What'd Jesus do? Would He burn with anger, or would He extend a hand of grace? When folks keep draggin' up your past like an old dog drags up a dead rabbit, it's a chance to show 'em what it means to be Christlike.

When those echoes start whisperin' old tales, don't let 'em rile you. Show 'em the old chapters have got a new twist, and there's a fresh ride ahead. Just like Jesus didn't back down from the rugged and the smooth, neither should we.

COWBOY CALL

You're going to lose people. It's not a sign that you're doing something wrong; sometimes it's because you're doing it right. The ones who can't see the new creation probably don't need to be a part of it. If they can't let it go, then let them go.

Never the Same Way Twice

Jesus saddled up again and rode away from the country around Tyre and headed through the area of Sidon on His way to the Sea of Galilee. Some fellows found Him and brought along a guy who was deaf and couldn't speak. They asked Jesus to put His hands on him and heal him. Jesus took him off to the side and put His fingers in the man's ears. Then He spit on His own fingers and touched the mute man's tongue. Jesus looked up to heaven and said quietly, "Open 'em up." Immediately, the man's ears were opened and his tongue was loosened.

MARK 7:31-35

Did you know that Jesus never healed people the same way twice? One time He spit on the ground, made a mud pie, and put it on a man's eyes to heal him. Here, He licks his fingers, puts them on the man's tongue, then sticks His fingers in his ears to heal him. Ever reckon that Jesus healed people in different ways because He had a deep understanding of how truly different each person was?

Similarly, not every person will be reached the same way. That preacher in the three-piece will reach people that I wouldn't even be allowed to preach to, but the same goes the other way too. It's crazy how we can claim to be a part of the family of God and then expect everyone to do, say, think, and act the exact same way.

God created us to be different—to have different experiences, different gifts and talents, different personalities, and to enjoy different hobbies. And you know what? He designed us to worship Him in different ways too. Some worship God by working tirelessly to build grand cathedrals, while others find Him in the quiet solitude of nature, beneath the starlit skies.

Just like the diverse landscapes of this great land we ride through, the diversity of His children is a testament to His creativity. Our unique paths to Him, our distinct ways of expressing our faith, should be celebrated, not judged.

What matters most is that we are all connecting to our Savior in our own ways, which should be the most important thing of all.

COWBOY CALL

When's the last time you did something different? Do you have a dream you'd like to follow, but you're afraid that others might not share your vision? Trust God and let Him work through you, even if it's unconventional. Just don't spit in anyone's eyes. You're not Jesus.

One Bad Apple

As they were on the trail, they had forgotten to get some provisions and just had one little old loaf of bread. Jesus used it as an illustration and said, "Y'all be careful. Beware of the yeast that infiltrates the biscuits of Herod and all them bigwig preachers."

MARK 8:14-18

You see, when Jesus refers to "yeast," He was saying there was something wrong about it. He was warning His followers to be on guard against the teachings of the Pharisees because it was tainted with hypocrisy, spiritual pride, and self-righteousness. The Pharisees paid a great deal of attention to outward ordinances and actions that would make them appear righteous, but they were not as concerned with actually being righteous in their hearts. Now, listen close, 'cause this here's a trail that's easy to stray from. When rules and restrictions, traditions and ceremonies become more important to you than your personal relationship with the Savior, it's like a fancy saddle that might seem real fine, but snaps if it's under any pressure. Jesus was right on the money when He warned us 'bout it.

Imagine you're gatherin' a bunch of cattle. Just one ornery critter can stir up a ruckus and make the whole bunch unruly. Same goes for religion. When we start fixatin' on traditions and ceremonies, we run the risk of lettin' it sneak into our hearts. It's like rust takin' over a fine piece of iron, and before you know it, our faith's all tarnished.

It's a trap, friends, a dangerous pitfall. We start thinkin' that all them rituals and doin's can lead us straight to God. But truth is, there's only one trail that leads us home—the one marked by the Son, Jesus Christ.

Don't be fooled by fancy saddles, and don't let ceremony cloud your vision. Hold on tight to the reins of a true faith, tied hard and fast to the love of the Savior.

COWBOY CALL

Which part of your faith seems to get monotonous? That's usually a sign that you're going through the motions instead of doing things for the right reasons.

Our salvation
is not a reward
of our deeds,
but a result of His

abundant grace
and our faith in
Jesus Christ.

"If I Can?"

"How long has this been going on?" Jesus asked.
The father replied, "Since he was just knee-high, this devil has been throwing my poor son in the water and even in the branding fire a time or two trying to kill him. I can't let him out of my sight, and I'm wore plumb out, Sir. Will You help us if You can?"
"What do you mean, 'If I can'?" Jesus raised an eyebrow and asked. "Ain't nothin' impossible for a man that believes."
The man fell to his knees and sobbed, "I want to believe, but You've got to help me!"

MARK 9:21-24

There is not a more vivid picture in my mind than Jesus's reply and the look on His face when this tormented father asked, "Will You help us if You can?"

To me, it's like asking a dog if it can lick. It's like asking a cat if it can purr or a lion if it can kill. I see a mixture of amusement, absolute confidence, and maybe even a little bit of sadness in Jesus's reaction.

"What do you mean, 'If I can'?"

Of course He can. He is the Son of God. He can do so much more than anything we could ever imagine, and yet sometimes we doubt Him. Sometimes we think He is too busy for us so we'll just handle it on our own. Sometimes we forget that the Creator of the entire universe is waiting on us to tag Him in.

The good news is that He is all-knowing, so He knows we will have our doubts, He knows we will forget, and He's not really bothered by it. And even better news? All we have to do is go to Him and ask Him to increase our belief so it will overrule our doubts. So when we don't have the hope we need to keep going but we believe Jesus can help us, He will come through—because *"Ain't nothin' impossible for a man that believes."*

Don't get me wrong, it's not that Jesus is some sort of genie granting wishes. Just because we believe doesn't beholden God to our wishes. But if we truly believe, we know that God is working on our behalf and we trust that His decision on how to answer our prayers is best.

Just remember, faith doesn't come from some sort of self-discipline. It comes from God, and the Bible says He can give us more. All we have to do is ask.

COWBOY CALL

Have you ever found yourself doubting God? Do the results you want affect how you feel about God? We must always remember that Jesus can and wants to be a part of our everyday lives. And He cares about our suffering, just like He cared about that daddy's tormented son. We just gotta believe . . . that *He can*!

THE MOTIVE BEHIND

Jesus nodded and added, "Listen, there ain't a cowboy alive who has left their home, their job, their family, or anything, or anyone, in order to ride with Me that won't get a hundred times back anything they think they've left. It won't be easy, but it'll all be worth it. But one thing to remember, those that ride the longest will be the last to ride through the gate. A good cowboy always makes sure everyone is through the gate before he gets off and shuts it."

MARK 10:29-31

Jesus is flat-out sayin' that following Him is worth it. You can never outgive God. Anything we give up for His sake will be rewarded a hundred times over.

But what's your real motive for following Christ?

A person following Christ to gain earthly riches, such as money, status, or the biggest ranch in three states, will probably never see the real benefits. That's because they still cannot understand that *He* is the reward. They're looking for substance instead of sustenance. They're looking for a meal to fill their bellies when Jesus is offering the bread of eternal life.

Let's follow Jesus not for what we can get, but for who He is—a Savior, a Friend, and the truest Treasure we could ever know. In Him, we find riches that the world could never match, and our journey with Him is worth every step. I often dream about what it will be like when one day I am face-to-face with Jesus. All those times I fretted about a stranger's comment on social media or why I lost friends will seem irrelevant. Every heartache, every tear, every prayer uttered will have all been worth it. The hard part about all this is that it's incomprehensible. We can't understand it now, but we will someday.

COWBOY CALL

What is your real motive for following Jesus? Have you ever truly thought about it? Is it because you've always gone to church? Or because being a Christian is the "right thing to do"? Ask God to show you any motive that isn't pure, and ask Him to purify your heart and intentions. Just as a cowboy must check the condition of his gear before embarking on a long ride, it's essential for us to inspect our spiritual motives and intentions regularly.

All Hat and No Cattle

The next morning they got up and rode out of Bethany. Jesus was hungry, and He saw a fig tree a little way off the trail. The tree was bright and full of life and leaves, but there were no figs, despite that it was a little early in the season. Jesus rode off from the tree and said loud enough for His cowboys to hear, "May you never make fruit again."

MARK 11:12-14

There's an old saying in the cowboy world: all hat and no cattle. This is someone who looks the part, but couldn't saddle a horse if their life depended on it.

When Jesus cursed the fig tree, He was basically saying the same thing. The tree was all leaves and no fruit. It looked good, but it was just taking up space and resources without doing anything useful.

When the Bible speaks of bearing fruit, it means your relationship with Christ is bringing about sweet refreshment in your life and in the lives of those around you. It means your life is resulting in a bountiful harvest of goodness, love, and righteousness. Now, that doesn't mean you have to make big gestures or stage huge events to bear a fruit the size of a pineapple. No, sometimes something as small as a blueberry can make a big difference. Jesus even said that something as small as a mustard seed could change the world.

This is a pretty stark revelation when you consider the current state of our Christian lives. Do we only look like good Christians, or are we bearing real fruit? Are we all hat and no cattle?

Having a bunch of leaves with no fruit is like wearing a mask and pretending that you're healthy. Trying to appear on the outside as if you are the perfect Christian does nothing for you—it's just leaves. But actually having a real relationship with Jesus, well . . . that's when you start to see the sweetest, most delightful results.

COWBOY CALL

Is your life bearing fruit? Here are some simple reminders on how to grow great fruit. Trees that are healthy don't have to struggle to bear fruit. They just do. It's not a chore for a healthy tree to make fruit. All you need is good soil (your environment), good light (the love of God), and good water (the Living Water). When you give your life to God and follow Him, you get all of that. Now, go make some good fruit.

What Will Heaven Be Like?

Jesus said to them, "Y'all ain't got a clue what you're talking about. Y'all don't know God's words from a cow turd. And you certainly don't know anything about the power of God. When people are raised from the dead and enter heaven, none of them will be married to anyone, but rather, they will be like the angels."

MARK 12:24-25

It's real hard for us to imagine what heaven will be like. In the verses above, it appears Jesus is saying that heaven will be much different from life as we know it on earth. While it seems we will be able to recognize fellow believers and family members who are in heaven, the purpose of heaven isn't to reunite us with those we loved—it's to reunite us with God.

Honestly, I don't want to take anything with me when I go. I'm happy to leave behind the pain and suffering that comes with being human. We will be united with our King, and He will care for us for all of eternity. Why would we want anything more than that?

Think about it—everything that is important to us on earth will no longer matter. No more bills, no more pain, no natural disasters, no need for a house or a truck or medicine. Maybe it's time we started living with heaven in mind, living with the freedom of knowing that no matter what happens here on earth, our reward is complete and total peace in the presence of our Savior.

COWBOY CALL

What would it mean for you to live with eternity in mind? Would you put more of a priority on your relationships? On sharing about God? Or maybe you would be more apt to let go of small squabbles and little bumps in the road and focus more on what is sure to be a wonderful existence forever and ever and ever.

God's New Home

As Jesus and His cowboys were leaving the church that day, one of 'em said, "Hey, Boss, look at how big and pretty this building is. Isn't it impressive?" Jesus replied, "You got that right. All these buildings are impressive, but not a single one will be left standing. They will all be knocked down."

MARK 13:1-2

While the Temple was an extraordinary building and the resting place of God on earth, Jesus said it would all be torn down. Why? Because after Jesus was sacrificed, God's residence on earth became our hearts, not a building. You see, when Jesus died, He took with Him the need for an earthly sanctuary because for the first time in human history since the Garden of Eden, people were able to have a personal relationship with God. People no longer had to visit the Temple (where God resided), give animal sacrifices, and rely on priests and prophets to tell them what God said.

While God used to reside in the Old Testament Temple, today He lives in our hearts through the Holy Spirit. Our souls are now the temple of God, and He resides there until we are reunited with Him in heaven.

I honestly have trouble with people calling a church building a "house of God." That's just not true. A building will never again be the home of God. Because God lives in us, we are His dwelling, meaning collectively, every single one of us who has called on Jesus as Lord and Savior is now the Church.

With this in mind, think about the other buildings you hold in high regard. Is it the actual structure, or is it the people in it that makes it special? The house that you've worked so hard for will one day be torn down. But the people in it can meet you in heaven. That truck you drive will end up in a junkyard eventually. But the early-morning conversations with your kiddos as you drive them to school could have an eternal impact. Even the tree you planted with your granddad will one day die and fall. But the time you spent with your granddad under its shade, learning life's lessons and sharing stories, could be a pivotal point in your faith story. The more we are aware of what truly holds significance to God, the more we will prioritize people over places.

COWBOY CALL

Do you take your role as the new home for God's Spirit seriously? Do you realize that all the power of God resides in us and is saving us as we speak? Take a moment today to put things, especially material things, in their proper place: after God and other people.

Talk Is Cheap

They all saddled up and rode off toward Gethsemane. When they got there, He told all the cowboys to wait there and pray. He motioned for Pete, James, and John to follow Him. Jesus looked worse than they'd ever seen Him, and He told them, "I want y'all to stay here with Me. I'm so full of dread that My heart feels like it's going to stop. Please keep Me company. I need y'all right now, pards." He got up and went back to where He'd left Pete, James, and John. They were all sound asleep. He woke Pete up and said, "Did you really fall asleep at a time like this? Keep a sharp lookout. Start praying so that you will not be ambushed by any sinful temptations. I know you want to do what's right, but talk is cheap."

MARK 14:32-34, 37-38

Jesus was praying in the Garden of Gethsemane and asked Peter, James, and John to stay awake while He went and prayed.

Peter had just got through saying that he would never deny Jesus and would stick with Him until the end. But Jesus comes back from praying and finds them all fast asleep.

Where is all the boasting that Peter had just done? Where's all the fire and brimstone he'd basically said he'd bring down on Jesus's enemies? Pete had basically just said that he'd fight a grizzly bear for Jesus, but he couldn't fight to stay awake on Jesus's last night on earth.

Don't be too hard on Pete, though. We do this all the time. We make big, boastful claims about following God, and then, within an hour, we aren't doing what we said we'd do. It's easy to make big promises, but delivering on 'em is more difficult. The good news is, Jesus doesn't hold our failures against us, especially if we talk to Him about them. Jesus just wants us to learn from the moment and move along. As long as we continue to pursue God, He will be by our side, strengthening and guiding us as we grow in our relationship with Christ.

So next time you break a promise you made to God, think about Peter, James, and John, and how guilty they must have felt about falling asleep that night. And then don't hesitate to humble yourself before God, let Him know you aren't proud of it, and then continue on your journey. That's all you're asked to do.

COWBOY CALL

Ever find yourself making the same promise to God over and over? And then breaking that same promise over and over? Don't give up! Keep talking to God, and keep leaning in. Jesus forgives all sins (even repeated ones). Remember Jesus is the Savior who forgives promise breakers when they repent and return to Him.

The First One Saved

During the feast of Flat Bread, and the celebration of Passover, it was a tradition to release one person who was in jail and awaiting execution. There was one particularly nasty fellow named Barabbas, who was locked up for murder. The crowd asked Pilate to release a prisoner, and he asked if they would rather release Jesus or Barabbas. Pilate said, "Do you want me to let the Boss of the Jews go?" But he knew the religious leaders were just jealous of Jesus. Pilate was stalling and trying to help Him all he could. The religious leaders stirred up the crowd against Jesus, and they lobbied to have Barabbas released instead.

MARK 15:6-11

Most of the time we miss this important part of Jesus's crucifixion. It was customary for a prisoner to be pardoned during the Passover celebration. Pilate was trying to get Jesus freed, but the crowds wouldn't have it. Some of the same folks who praised Jesus with palm branches when He rode into Jerusalem on a colt were now calling for His death! They only lobbied to have Barabbas freed because they wanted Jesus killed.

If you think about it, Barabbas was the first one to benefit from Jesus's sacrifice. Jesus was handed over to free Barabbas. A guilty person was let go, and an innocent man was marked for death. People usually say the thief on the cross was the first one saved, but I think Barabbas was saved first when he was released. I wonder what he did with the rest of his life.

This begs the question: Jesus freed us, too, so what are we doing with our newfound freedom? Do we continue to live as we did before, or do we scratch out a new trail toward a new destination—a destination that is perfect and waiting on all who would seek it and give anything for it? As a matter of fact, the price is everything. That's the price we pay for our new freedom.

And when we finally find the courage to pay the price, we realize that it's the least we could do for what we gain. We get peace for eternity, and all we have to do is give Jesus our pitiful little lives. It's a great deal for us.

Jesus went to the cross to be punished for your sins, or wrongdoings, so you could be free like Barabbas. What will you do with your newfound freedom?

COWBOY CALL

God adds value to our lives that wasn't there before. He takes our sins and makes us perfect in His sight. He takes our pain and offers us peace. Whenever God takes things from our lives, it always makes us more valuable, not less. How do you see yourself through God's eyes?

Going In

When the Day of Rest was over, the women brought spices to embalm Jesus's body. It was very early on Sunday morning, and they worried about how they were going to move the heavy stone that had been placed in front of the tomb. But when they got to the tomb, the stone had already been rolled away. They walked into the tomb to take care of Jesus's body, but all they saw was a man sitting to the right of where they had laid Him. This shocked them, and they didn't know what to do or what to say. But the man said to them, "Whoa! Don't be scared, ladies. You are looking for Jesus of Nazareth, but He ain't here. This is where His body was placed, but like I said, He ain't here. Go tell Jesus's cowboys, especially Pete, that Jesus is heading for Galilee and said to meet Him there."

MARK 16:2-7

Jesus rose from the dead three days after His crucifixion, just like He said He would. While He told parables and illustrations to explain many things, this wasn't just a story. He really did rise from the grave.

One of the most powerful stories I've ever heard about the resurrection of Christ was why the stone was rolled away. It wasn't rolled away so Jesus could come out. It was rolled away so we could come out.

Because of what Jesus did, we can approach our own "tombs"—the places of our deepest fears and greatest challenges—with faith in God's power to overcome. When we are faced with problems that seem insurmountable, much like the large stone blocking the tomb, let us remember that God is bigger than anything that might stand in our way. And He has a plan for us, even when things don't make a lot of sense.

When will you leave all your shame, worries, and problems in the tomb? Isn't it time to walk out of the cave, surrender those things to our almighty God, and leave them behind?

COWBOY CALL

The empty tomb symbolizes Jesus's victory over death, the ultimate manifestation of God's power. In our lives, this translates to the promise that no matter what we face, God's power is greater. The angel's message, "He ain't here," is a call to remember that God's plans are often beyond our comprehension. We may anticipate one outcome, only to find that God has a far better one in store.

Long in the Tooth

Then an angel appeared right next to the table where Zechariah was offering incense. The sight of the angel nearly toppled old Zechariah. He started shaking like a leaf. But the angel told him, "Whoa, amigo. Don't let me spook ya. I've come to tell ya that God has been listening to your prayers, and your wife will give birth to a baby boy. God wants you to name him John . . . He's going to be a top hand for the Lord . . . the Holy Spirit will be with him. John's going to gather a lot of people for God's outfit. He's going to get everything ready for when the Lord comes . . . He will . . . show people who are not riding for God how to change the way they do things."
Zechariah lowered his gaze and asked, "How can I believe this? The wife and I are real long in the tooth."
The angel said, "My name is Gabriel, and I stand before God, always ready to do His, and only His bidding. He sent me here to bring you this good news . . . You didn't believe what I said, so you are no longer going to be able to speak until all that I have told you comes to pass . . . and it will."

LUKE 1:11-13, 15-20

This is the only story of John the Barbarian Baptist's birth. We don't hear anything else about Zechariah after this passage, but that doesn't mean he didn't play a huge part in the Gospel story.

Much like Abraham and Sarah, Zechariah and his wife were long in the tooth and never had any kids. They prayed their whole lives for a child, but then when an actual angel tells them their prayers are fixing to come true, Zechariah doubts it.

Has this ever happened to you? You've prayed and prayed for something to happen, and when things start heading in that direction, you don't want to believe it. Maybe because you don't want to get your hopes up; You don't want to jinx it. Whatever the case may be, you had the faith to pray the big prayers, but for some reason, you are having a hard time believing God is big enough to come through.

Well, let me be the first to tell you—God is big enough; He is all-powerful and unstoppable; and He is working in your life. You can bet on it.

COWBOY CALL

God hears our prayers when we don't give up. And it can be kinda scary when the God of everything answers your prayers. I can't tell you how many times I've seen folks get their prayers answered, and when I ask them how they feel, they tell me they're scared to death. If you have the faith to pray, have the faith to accept the answers. What have you given up praying for?

We don't find Jesus. Jesus finds us. It is a beautiful moment when we realize the presence of Christ

in our lives,
not because
we have suddenly
found Him,
but because
He sought us out.

Not Everyone Will Believe

There was an old cowboy living in Jerusalem named Simeon. He'd been waiting for the day when God would send His Top Hand... The Holy Spirit had told the old cowboy that he wouldn't die before he had seen God's Top Hand. The Spirit guided old Simeon to the main church in Jerusalem. It was no coincidence because after he arrived there, Joseph and Mary showed up with Jesus to do what the Code of Moses instructed. Simeon took one look at the baby and said, "Now I can die and go to God in peace. I've done seen with my own eyes how You will save everyone. Now everyone will know Your plan. This boy will be a light for all men and all nations, and He will bring honor and glory to Israel." Now Joseph and Mary were stunned by what the old cowboy said. Simeon blessed the parents and then said to Mary, "This boy will be the saving and undoing of many. Not everyone will believe in Him. He will reveal the hearts of all people... The things that will come will bring you much pain—it'll be like a blade through your heart."

LUKE 2:25-35 CV

Old Simeon knew the truth: not everyone would believe in Jesus, but His presence on this earth was going to reveal the hearts of people, meaning that those who encountered Jesus would be faced with a choice— to accept the salvation He brought or to turn it away.

So, how do you know if you truly believe? If your belief in Jesus doesn't radically change your life or influence your decisions, you might want to give it a good once-over.

How do we know what to believe? The Good Book tells us. We can't just believe what it says; we must trust in what it says as well as obey. Now, there's several of us cowboys who don't like the word *obey*. We want to go our own way and do our own thing. But when it comes to living each day with Jesus—living with His grace, kindness, care, and companionship—once you walk throuh life with Him, you really don't ever want to walk without Him. So when we talk about "obeying" in this sense, we are really just talking about our response to His goodness. It's not a forced march, it's a natural outpouring of our heart's gratitude. It's not about following a set of rigid rules; it's about willingly surrendering your will to His.

COWBOY CALL

Simeon waited patiently, and when the time came, he got to see the promised Messiah. What if he hadn't obeyed that day? He'd have missed out on seeing Jesus. Ever skipped a calling and missed a major chance? Don't repeat the same mistake! Always follow through, despite discomfort or inconvenience, because you never know what potential blessings are waiting for you on the other side.

Jesus Is Dunked

While everyone was in line to get dunked by John, Jesus came too. After getting dunked, Jesus was praying, and the whole sky opened up. The Holy Spirit flew down from heaven in the form of a dove and landed on Him. Then from heaven, a voice shook the earth as it said, "You are My boy, and You sure make a Dad proud."

LUKE 3:21-22

Baptism expresses a recognition of Christ's death and resurrection—the old self was crucified with Christ, and now followers of Jesus have risen with Him in "newness of life" (Romans 6:3–11 NASB). But Jesus never had an "old self" that needed to be made new, so why was He baptized? Jesus's baptism represented the beginning of His mission to bring redemption to the world. It is a reminder that, although He had no "old self" to crucify and renew, He willingly took on the form of a servant and immersed Himself in the human experience, setting a model of righteousness, selflessness, and obedience. Basically, Jesus lived to show us how to live. His baptism was an act of obedience, setting an example for us to follow.

Have you ever looked at how Jesus lived when He walked the earth? How He treated people with love and compassion? How He responded to those He disagreed with—with grace and wisdom? How He prioritized quiet time to talk to His Father?

Maybe it's time we start striving to model our own lives after His, following in His footsteps. While we will never be perfect, like Jesus is, we can sure try.

COWBOY CALL

The voice from heaven that tells Jesus, "You sure make a Dad proud" immediately after His baptism offers a powerful declaration of Jesus's identity and worth, showing us that our identity should be tied hard in God's love for us and His adoption of us as His children. This adoption is not based on our works, but on our relationship with Him. Have you been baptized? It's never too late, you know.

The Invisible Messiah

Then Jesus rode over the hills and to His old stomping grounds of Nazareth. On the Day of Rest, He went like always to the local church. He stood up to read out of the Good Book and turned to Isaiah. He scanned through the verses and then read, "God's Spirit is riding with Me. He has sent Me to bring the Good News to the poor. I will make a way for those held captive to be let loose, and I will make the blind see. Those that are oppressed will now have a champion. I will announce that the time is now when the Lord will save His people."
Jesus shut the book, handed it back, and sat down. Everyone in church was staring at Him, and you could've heard a pin drop. With all their eyes locked on Him, He looked up and said, "All I read has come true today."

LUKE 4:16-21

This passage tells of Jesus's visit to his hometown of Nazareth, where He went to the synagogue on the Sabbath and read a passage from the book of Isaiah. The passage, which prophesied the coming of a servant of God who would bring good news to the poor, freedom for the prisoners, recovery of sight for the blind, and deliverance for the oppressed, was then claimed by Jesus as being fulfilled by Him that very day.

But the people missed it. When Jesus came, He wasn't what they expected. He wasn't some warrior who came to free Israel from Roman oppression. He was God, dressed and clothed as a simple man, who came to free them from sin.

Have you ever dismissed someone due to the way they were dressed or spoke? What about the city slicker who showed up at the honky-tonk? Or the hippie who came to church without any shoes? Just as the people of Nazareth initially failed to recognize Jesus as the Messiah because He didn't fit their preconceived notions, we, too, can sometimes miss the extraordinary in the ordinary.

The truth is, a lot of times God chooses the least expected to accomplish His work. Let us strive to see people as God sees them, regardless of how they appear. Let's not allow what could be a God-initiated appointment slip by us because we can't get past our own prejudices.

COWBOY CALL

Those of us who ride for Christ are called to bring good news, to help free those in bondage, to bring healing, and to share God's love and blessings with everyone we meet—not just the ones who look and talk like us, but with everyone.

A New Purpose

Pete told Him, "Sir, we fished out there all night and didn't catch nothing. But if You say so, we'll go out again." When they did, they caught so many fish that their nets started tearing apart. They hollered for some help, and soon other boats' nets were so full that they, too, began to nearly sink. When Pete finally caught on to what was happening, he hit one knee before Jesus and said, "Lord, You've got to ride away from here. I'm not worthy enough to be within Your sight." His heart was beating fast with amazement at what he'd just experienced. James and John, his other partners, were also amazed. Jesus smiled and said, "Don't be afraid of being with Me. You're gonna come with Me, and I'm going to help you go from catching fish to gathering strays." When the boat got back to shore, they saddled up, left everything behind, and rode off with Jesus.

LUKE 5:5-11

Peter, an experienced fisherman, might have been skeptical when Jesus, a carpenter turned preacher, asked him to let down the nets again after a whole night of failure. However, he did what Jesus said, and they caught so many fish that their nets started breaking and they needed help from another boat. Seeing the miracle, Peter was overwhelmed and confessed his unworthiness in the presence of Jesus. However, Jesus comforted him and gave him a new purpose: to share the Gospel and be a "fisher of men," or a "gatherer of strays."

Jesus reassures us, too, that our past, our shortcomings, and our feelings of unworthiness do not disqualify us from riding for Him. Instead, like Pete, we are called to leave behind our old lives and follow Him. Jesus transforms our lives, giving us new purpose and direction.

This passage is a powerful illustration of Jesus's power. It also underscores the importance of obedience and faith. Despite their doubts and previous failures, the future disciples obeyed Jesus and were rewarded abundantly.

COWBOY CALL

In our old lives, our purpose was pretty much living day to day and preparing for tomorrow. When we come to follow Christ, we learn to live every day and prepare for eternity. The Good Book says that Jesus told them they would go from being fishermen to fishers of men. God takes what we are good at and leads us to a new purpose—a Kingdom purpose. What if we worked just as hard on preparing for eternity as we do on paying the light bill and feeding our families? One will be fruitless tomorrow, but the other will be fruitful for eternity.

Trials and Trails

Jesus continued, "It's going to be rough going for those of you who ride for Me. You'll be hated, insulted, and even shut out because of your decision. But when this happens, you will be blessed. Even in the darkest of these moments, you can smile because your reward in heaven will outweigh any problem down here. And you aren't alone in your trials and trails. They did the same things to God's hands while they rode down here."

LUKE 6:22-23

Jesus surprises His cowboys when He tells them that they're blessed when people hate, exclude, insult, and reject them because of Him. Jesus encourages them to rejoice in these situations because their reward in heaven is great. He reminds them that this is similar to how the old cowboys from the Old Testament were treated in the past.

This illustrates why following Jesus is different. Jesus says that those who face persecution for their faith aren't to be pitied because they're actually blessed. This is a radical departure from the world's view, that happiness and blessings come from popularity, acceptance, and earthly success.

Jesus is emphasizing that the Kingdom of God operates on different values. He's preparing His disciples for the inevitable hardship and persecution they will face as they live out their faith. But He comforts them with the assurance that their reward in heaven far outweighs any earthly suffering.

We need to remain steadfast and joyful in the face of getting mucked out. We need to remember that true blessings and rewards come from God, not from human approval or earthly success. Even when faced with rejection or persecution, we can rejoice, knowing that we're following in the footsteps of the prophets and that God will greatly reward us.

COWBOY CALL

We all want God's best plan: get God, get rich, get healed, get fed, get forgiven, and get eternity. While there are eternal benefits to God's plan, we often forget just how hard it will be. I've always said that anyone can claim they're tough, but I want to be there when you smash your finger with a hammer. It's easy to say that you follow Christ during a Sunday service that's rich and enlightening; it's another story to follow Him when you're heartbroken and damaged.

Religious Hypocrisy

Then Jesus said, "Let Me see if I can explain the folks of this generation. They are like the fans in the stands while the cowboys stand in the arena and talk to them. The cowboys say to them, 'We rode the rough stock for you and got bucked off, but you didn't cheer because you wanted to see us rope. We roped fast and quick, but you didn't clap because no one got bucked off.' John didn't drink alcohol and often went without food so he could pray, but y'all said he was evil. But then God's Top Hand comes having a beer with outlaws and whores, but y'all say, 'He's a pig and a drunk, and He hangs out with lowlifes.' Wisdom is found in the truth, not in someone's opinion."

LUKE 7:31-35

In this passage, Jesus compares His generation to children who are never satisfied with anything. He likens them to children sitting at a rodeo who are unhappy no matter what: they complain that the bronc riding is too long and the roping is too boring.

He says they make the rules and then complain when nobody follows their rules. But the rules were rigged—there was no way to win. Even though both John the Barbarian Baptist and Jesus lived opposite, "holy" lives, they were both condemned.

They accused John of having a demon because he didn't eat bread or drink wine. Yet, they also criticized Jesus, who did eat and drink, accusing Him of being a friend of tax collectors and sinners.

People's judgment and their refusal to accept God's work, no matter how it's presented, is fickle at best. Whether it was John's seriousness or Jesus's sociability, the people found reasons to dismiss and criticize them both.

Maybe this is a call for self-examination of our attitudes. Are we like the spoiled children, never satisfied and always criticizing? Or are we open to God's work in whatever form it takes? The message of God and His servants often defies people's expectations and cannot be confined to their preconceived notions. We should look past superficial judgments and accept God's work in our lives, even if it's unconventional.

COWBOY CALL

John was as devout as a person could be, but he wasn't controlled by the whims and standards of men. The same can be said of Jesus, who also wasn't controlled by the ever-changing standards of other people. Jesus wasn't telling us to choose His way or John's; He was exposing religious hypocrisy.

Owning Up

Jesus turned and asked, "Who touched Me?"
Everyone turned around all innocent like, and then Pete said, "Boss, there's a bunch of people. Maybe someone accidentally bumped Ya."
But Jesus replied, "I felt the healing power leave Me. Someone touched Me on purpose."
The woman was real scared now, and she trembled as she took a knee before Jesus. She then explained why she had touched His vest and how she had immediately been cured.
Jesus smiled kindly at her and said, "Daughter, your faith in Me has healed you. Go in peace!"

LUKE 8:45-48

This is about a woman who'd been ailing for a dozen years. While she'd spent all her money on doctors, they couldn't help her. She was in a real pickle. Then one day as Jesus was walkin' through a crowd of people, she touched the hem of His robe, believin' that'd be enough to heal her. And you know what? It was.

Jesus turned around and asked, "Who touched Me?" His cowboys thought He was loco, sayin', "Master, this crowd's pushin' and shovin', but You ask, 'Who touched Me?'"

But Jesus insisted, "Someone touched Me; I know that power has gone out from Me." Then the woman, seeing that she couldn't remain hidden, came trembling and fell at His feet. She expected to be rebuked, but instead, she found grace.

In front of everybody, she declared why she'd touched Him and how she'd been instantly healed. Jesus said to her, "Daughter, your faith has healed you. Go in peace."

Just like that woman, we've all got hurts that need healin', maybe not physical, but hurts all the same. And just like her, all we need to do is reach out in faith to Jesus. So, saddle up and ride with Him, because with faith, there's healing in His touch.

COWBOY CALL

Do you really think Jesus didn't know who touched Him? I believe He did. What He wanted was not just to heal the woman, but for her to come face-to-face with Him. He wanted her to know that while He is powerful, He is also good. Many times, we want the anonymous healing or answered prayer. We want what God offers, but we don't want to come face-to-face with Him. When was the last time you bared your soul, stood in front of the Almighty, and said, "I am here"?

Shake the Dust from Your Boots

Jesus called His twelve cowboys to Him and told 'em to listen up. He gave 'em all power to whip demons and cure cankers and cancers. He then sent them out to tell everyone the Good News about God's outfit. He told 'em, "Just take what you need and nothing else. Don't take a packhorse or even saddlebags. Don't stick any money into the bottom of your boots for emergency, and don't even take your slicker. When people are glad to see you, stay at their place until you leave. If people are unfriendly toward you, then leave that ranch and shake the dust off your boots, so you don't spread their hate around."

LUKE 9:1-5

Jesus gathered His cowboys and gave 'em power and authority to drive out demons and heal diseases. Then He sent 'em out to preach the Kingdom of God and heal the sick.

He told 'em, "Take nothin' for the journey. No saddlebags, no bread, no money, not even an extra shirt. Whatever ranch you go to, stay there until you leave that area. If folks don't welcome you, shake the dust off your boots when you leave, as a testimony against 'em."

Now, that's a real cowboy mission, ain't it? We have been called to saddle up and ride out, preachin' the Good News and bringin' relief. We ain't supposed to worry 'bout provision or acceptance. Our job's to deliver the message.

Jesus has given each of us the authority and the power we need to fulfill the specific purposes He has placed on our lives—to fulfill our individual Kingdom missions. We just gotta trust Him and go where He leads. And if folks don't take kindly to the message, we ain't supposed to go to raking folks with our spurs. We should just shake the dust off our boots and move on. Remember, it ain't about us; it's about Him.

COWBOY CALL

Nobody likes having rocks thrown at them—verbally, visually, or physically. But Jesus just tells His cowboys to shake the dust off their boots and move on. Not everyone is going to like you or what you say. This doesn't make it feel any better; it's just a fact. There's an old quote by Winston Churchill that goes something like, "You'll never get where you're going if you stop and throw rocks at every dog that barks." We need to learn to just move on. How do we do that? By practicing moving on. Keep going in the direction that God told you to go and don't look back.

Smart As a Kid

At that moment, the Holy Spirit filled Jesus with joy, and He prayed, "Boss, You're Lord over heaven and this big ball of dirt and water. Thank You for hiding the truth from those who think they are smart and showing it to those who have a childlike faith in You. I know this was Your plan, Dad, and I know You like it."

LUKE 10:21

The big truths of this universe ain't always revealed to the high and mighty—the so-called wise and learned. Nope, they're given to those humble enough to receive 'em like innocent children.

It's a bit like riding bucking horses. Some might think it's all about strength—about being the toughest one in the pen. But for those who have been there and done that, it's more about balance and trust. It's about being humble enough to move with the bronc rather than against it. It's about placing your trust in something bigger and stronger than you, about being wise enough to move with the wild and unpredictable bronc rather than struggling against it.

Same goes for us when we're dealing with God's truths. We learn to navigate the turbulence of life by humbling ourselves, finding balance, and placing our trust in the hands of something greater than ourselves. In doing so, we might just experience the deepest peace known to mankind.

COWBOY CALL

One Sunday after I finished preaching, two young girls who were no more than six or seven years old came up to me. One of them shyly asked, "Mr. Kevin, how do you know all that stuff?" I've been asked a lot of difficult questions in my life, but it seems like the ones from kids are the hardest. I took a second to formulate my answer, then said, "Well, I read all the time, I study nearly every day, and I try to pray constantly." She smiled real big at me and said, "Oh, I was wondering if that's how you did it." The other little girl was just itching to say something, so I turned to her and asked, "What is it, honey?" She was super proud of herself as she said, "You should try to practice too."

"God's Spirit
is riding with Me.
He has sent Me
to bring
the Good News
to the poor.
I will make a way
for those

held captive
to be let loose,
and I will make the
blind see.
Those that are
oppressed will
now have a
champion."

The Keys to Prayer

Then He gave them a clinic on prayer and said, "Let's say you eat the last of the food you have in your house and some company shows up. You run over to the neighboring ranch and knock on the door. A cowboy opens it and asks what you want so late, and you ask to borrow a bag of beans to feed your visitor. He shuts the door in your face and tells you to leave because everyone is asleep. But I'll say this, if you keep knocking on that door, he will give you a bag of beans just to make you go away. Persistence and boldness are the keys to prayer."

LUKE 11:5-8

This here's a story 'bout persistence. Jesus is sayin' not to be afraid to keep on knockin', even when it seems like the door's slammed shut. It's a bit like roping. You're going to miss, but the good thing about a rope is that it always has another loop in it.

Same goes for our prayers to the Good Lord. We gotta keep prayin' and keep askin' with a boldness that won't quit. Sometimes, it ain't about the friendship—it's about the persistence—the *keep on keeping on*. So, cowboys and cowgirls, let's keep knockin', keep prayin', and keep trustin' in the Lord's provision.

COWBOY CALL

I've often said that if you can't pray for something consistently, then you either don't want it bad enough or you don't need it. Too often, we give up way too soon on our prayers. Just think about how your kids hound you about something they want. They're relentless! That is how our prayers should be. But in addition to persistence, we need to add boldness. I have to remember that it takes no more effort for God to answer a big prayer than it does for Him to answer a little one. Pray big prayers and don't give up.

Petty Disputes over Stuff

Someone in the crowd hollered out, "Boss, tell my brother to split the cow herd with me that our father left us!" Jesus turned to him and said, "I'm not here to settle your petty disputes." Then He said to everyone, "Beware of the greed of material wealth. True life cannot be measured by what you have in your pastures."

LUKE 12:13-15

Have you ever noticed how Jesus seems to be tough sometimes? I love that about Him.

In Luke 12:13–15, Jesus makes it clear that He was not going to get into the middle of a family dispute about money. Jesus was and still is more interested in our character and eternal trajectory. You see, Jesus offers us *eternal life* in exchange for Him taking care of us and loving us every day. Yeah, read that again. He says (paraphrase mine), "If you give your life to Me and let Me protect, provide for, and guide you every single day, I'll build you a place in heaven." And some folks' response is, "That's not fair because that's not going to give me what I want right now."

Greed and material possessions can blind you. It's easy to focus on how much money you have (or how much money you think you should have) or to get caught up in disputes with those you feel cheated you financially. But to Jesus, the issue isn't whether or not you were swindled out of money or power; the issue is whether or not you handled that offense with character and grace.

COWBOY CALL

A church was fixing to split because one deacon couldn't get along with the pastor. Another pastor came in as a kind of mediator. He listened to the accusations and examples of wrongdoing on both sides. It came out that the dispute all began when the pastor didn't shake the deacon's hand one Sunday morning. That's when the moderator said, "Let's pray. Father in heaven, we come to You in the name of Jesus to ask us not to be stupid. Amen." The mediator got up and walked out. That church is still together. I don't know if God laughs at prayers, but I'm sure that one made Him grin.

Before It's Too Late

Jesus continued teaching in villages and cow camps on His way to Jerusalem. Someone once asked Him, "How many will end up on God's ranch?" He replied, "You need to try hard to get on with God's outfit before it's too late. Many will want on, but only a few will be chosen. When the Boss shuts the gate, it will be too late. You will stand outside and beg and plead, but the Boss will say, 'I will not. You're not one of My cowboys.' Then you'll say, 'But I went to one of Your clinics and even ate with Your cowboys.' And He will say, 'Get away from Me. I offered you a place a long time ago, and you refused. The gate has been open all this time for anyone who wanted to come in, but now it's too late. Get away from here and get away from Me.' When you finally realize the ranch you will spend eternity on, you will be in such severe pain that you will cry out and gnash your teeth as you suffer endlessly. You'll look across the fence and see... all of the old cowboys who rode for God. They'll be happy on God's outfit, but you'll never step foot on it."

LUKE 13:22-29

I love how Jesus never answers anyone's questions, not because He's contrary, but because the answer He gives always refers to the question they should have asked.

Here in this passage, they ask how many will end up in heaven, and Jesus answers with, "Get in the gate before it's too late." In many Bible translations, Jesus speaks of a "narrow door," or a challenging path, that leads to eternal life. This passage reminds us that the journey of faith, much like the rugged trails we ride and the obstacles we face, isn't always easy, but it's worth every step. The way to eternal life may not be easy, but if we face the treacherous terrain with determination, resilience, and faith, it will lead us to heaven. And that, my hombres, is worth every effort.

COWBOY CALL

The trouble with waiting to follow God is that all that waiting makes your heart hard. We can choose God's way, which is steep, rough, and narrow . . . or we can choose the wide road to destruction. Stay strong, cowboy, and keep riding the trail. Remember that the ultimate destination is worth every ounce of perseverance.

A "Manner" of Humility

As people were sitting down to eat, Jesus noticed how everyone was trying to get the best spots near the head of the table. Jesus said, "When you are eating at a branding and lunch is served, don't run in and try to sit at the table with the rancher. You take your plate and go outside to eat. It would be much better for you to have the rancher come outside and insist that you sit with him than him have to ask you to go sit outside. Then you'd be all kinds of embarrassed, and you'd have brought it on yourself. A wannabe who tries to pass himself off as a top hand will be humiliated, but the top hand who doesn't mind sitting outside will be given a place of honor."

LUKE 14:7-11

For those who aren't cowboys, this is a great example of what really happens. You go to eat, and if you watch closely, the best hands will go through the line and then take a seat somewhere that's the least comfortable or convenient. It might be in the sun when there are a few seats in the shade. They might sit on the bed of the truck instead of taking one of the few chairs.

But here's something else that happens.

Many times, the rancher or the cow boss will look up at his top hand who's sitting in the sun and tell him to come sit at the table in the shade with him. This is what Jesus will do for us when we reach heaven. We'll have a seat of honor at that table in heaven because we took the sorry seats down here.

A word of warning, though. I've seen many Christians make a big deal about how humble they are. My ranch hands and I have a running joke whenever someone starts bragging about something. They'll let them brag for a minute and then say, "And it's hard being the humblest guy that ever lived, isn't it?"

It's a small way of celebrating each other and then pushing each other back down the slide.

COWBOY CALL

There's nothing more humiliating than making a bad mistake in manners. Contrarily, there is nothing more gratifying than being praised when you least expect it or want it. Jesus is teaching a spiritual lesson here: trying to look like a big shot will get you shot down, but putting yourself last is the quickest way to coming in first. Don't look to honor yourself; instead use any opportunity to honor others. Don't talk about yourself; use the opportunity to speak well of others.

The Prodigal Son

"But the dad hollered to the cowboys who were working near the barn, 'Hey! Someone grab my best coat out of the house and put it on my son. Get a ring for his finger and boots for his feet. Butcher the grain-fed steer and get ready for a party. We are going to celebrate the return of my son to the ranch. He was once dead to us, but now he has returned to life! He was lost, but now he has been found!' Everyone started getting ready for the celebration to begin."

LUKE 15:22-24

In this passage, a son takes his inheritance before his dad dies and runs off for fame, fortune, women, and rock 'n' roll. He becomes destitute and finds himself in a bad way. He returns home hoping to be just a servant in his father's house. Instead, the father welcomes him back with loving arms. This parable is known as the story of "the prodigal son."

But not very many people know what "prodigal" means. It means "to spend money or resources freely and recklessly; to be wastefully extravagant." While this could very well summarize how the boy lived, I think it speaks more of the father's nature.

The father loved his son freely and recklessly and very extravagantly. It's more of a picture of God's love for us, that no matter what we've done, we will always have a place in His home. And not only do we have a place, but our return will be celebrated. We will be given gifts, and a meal will be prepared in our honor.

Do you feel as if you are too far gone to turn back to God? Trust me, you're not. There is nothing you can do, nothing you can say, nothing that can keep you from His love. All you have to do is talk to Him. Give it all to Him and let Him handle the details. He is waiting with his best coat in hand, a ring for your finger, and a party in your honor—ready for you to start walking back to Him.

COWBOY CALL

There's another very valuable spiritual lesson here. It's so easy to focus on the sins of both sons in this parable instead of the love of the father. Too often, we marinate in our own thoughts about the sorry deeds we've done instead of focusing on the love of the Father. We are not identified by the sins we commit, but by the relationship we have with our Father.

It's the Little Things

"If you can be trusted with little things, more will be trusted to you. If you cannot be trusted with small tasks, you cannot be trusted with bigger ones. If you are untrustworthy with things of this world, do you think God is going to trust you with the secrets of heaven? If you can't take care of other people's things, why should you be given more things of your own?"

LUKE 16:10-12

Years ago, I had a person come up to me and want to get involved in our ministry. I explained different ways he could do that, from helping set up for our Sunday clinics to helping build a fence at the ranch.

He was gung ho when he left, but I never saw him setting up or building any fence.

Time went by, and he approached me again and said, "I don't want to do any of that stuff. I just want to be one of the leaders."

I kindly informed him that I wanted the same thing, but I had showed him the trail that leads to leadership; it's a trail called serving.

We all want the big things in life. We want the grand things that come from following God, but it's being faithful in the little things that gets us there.

We want big ministries where thousands are saved, but we don't want to go check on a neighbor who has fallen ill. We pray for a big healing for a loved one, but we forget the little prayers for the people who don't seem important.

We've all done it.

But if you want more out of the life God has given you, He's not going to give you more until you do what He's already asked you to do . . . and He's very patient.

COWBOY CALL

When was the last time you served your family? Your community? Your church? Or anybody? We can get so caught up in our own worlds and tasks that it's easy to forget to look up and around at the needs of others. Keep your eyes open today to the needs of others, and if you feel led, make a plan to meet those needs. Maybe that means building a handicap ramp for your neighbor or volunteering at a homeless shelter. Whatever you do, remember it's the little things that count.

The Hard Truth

Then the twelve cowboys said, "Show us how to have more faith!" Jesus answered, "If you had the faith of an alfalfa seed, you could tell that oak tree, 'Climb out of the ground and go plant yourself in the bottom of the ocean,' and it would do what you said. When a cowboy comes in from checking fence, does the ranch owner tell him, 'Let me unsaddle your horse and rub it down while you go in and get something to eat?' No, he tells him, 'Go milk the cow and bring it to me while I eat supper. After that, then you can go eat.' Does the ranch owner praise the cowboy for doing his job? Of course not. In the same way, when you ride for Me, you should say, 'We're just happy to ride for You and do what You tell us to do.'"

LUKE 17:5-10

Do you believe Jesus? In this passage, He says, "If you had the faith of an alfalfa seed, you could tell that oak tree, 'Climb out of the ground and go plant yourself in the bottom of the ocean,' and it would do what you said."

Do you believe that? Is your faith big enough to believe that the impossible is possible? Jesus is saying that even with a small amount of faith, we can do big things! God-sized things! World-changing things!

Moving an oak tree? Simple as roping the dummy.

In Luke 17:5–10, Jesus is asked by His cowboys how to have such a world-changing faith. And one of His responses was: “Does the ranch owner praise the cowboy for doing his job? Of course not.” Now, this may sound harsh, but if we think about it, does God really owe us anything for our work? Is God the One who should be thankful, or is it us? It’s time we realize that if God didn’t ever do one thing more than send His Son to die on the cross, it would have been too much.

We need to start realizing that we ride for the Lord of lords and the King of kings. Just the opportunity to ride for His Brand is more than enough reward. But because God is good, He makes us sons and daughters of His own that He’ll never forsake and always love.

God doesn’t owe us anything, yet we owe Him everything.

COWBOY CALL

With God we are going to do amazing things, it’s true, but don’t start thinking you deserve those amazing things, or that you’re entitled to His blessings, or even that you have a right to all He has in store for you. Because you don’t. It doesn’t mean that He doesn’t see and appreciate your efforts; it just means all the service we could ever do for Christ pales in comparison to what He has done for us.

The Crooked Brand Inspector

Then Jesus told 'em this story of a guy who depended on his own goodness and shunned everyone else: "Two guys went into the church to pray. One was a religious fellow, and the other was a brand inspector. The religious fellow thought he was better than other people, so he stayed away from everyone else and prayed, 'Thank You, God, for not making me like the lowlife cheaters, sinners, and fornicators. And a special thank You for not making me like that crooked brand inspector over there. God, I go without food twice a week, and I tithe religiously.' But the crooked brand inspector stood a far piece away from everyone else because he didn't feel worthy. He wouldn't even look at heaven as he prayed. Instead, he dug his fingernails into his palm as he prayed, 'God, I'm a sorry piece of work. Please take me onto Your outfit even though we both know I don't deserve it.'" Jesus continued, "I'm telling you the truth, cowboys, this crooked brand inspector was right in God's eyes, not that religious fellow. Those who pat themselves on their backs will end up flat on their backs. And those who cry out to God with their faces down in sorrow will be lifted up to heaven."

LUKE 18:9-14

So you can ride rank broncs or tie hard and fast while roping renegade yearling bulls? That's not what makes you tough. The toughest cowboys are those who can see themselves for what they really are. That takes real strength.

Which guy do you most identify with in the passage at the top of this devotion? The religious fellow or the crooked brand inspector? Are you someone who shows up every time the door is open to the church, but you tend to look down on people who aren't like you? Do you think you're better than others?

Or are you the crooked brand inspector? Do you feel uncomfortable talking to God about where you've been and what you've done? Are you aware that your only hope is Jesus?

Most of us are somewhere in between these two characters, but Jesus makes it clear that we need to be more like the brand inspector. He knew that he fell short, while the religious fellow considered himself worthy of God's grace.

Take a close look at yourself today, and we'll see how tough you really are.

COWBOY CALL

Self-righteousness in the Kingdom of God is totally contrary to the way God wants us to live. When was the last time you truly cried out to God because of the things you've done? Are you still doing them?

When God Stood Among You

When Jesus got closer to the city, His eyes filled with tears. He said, "You, Jerusalem, have cried out to God for help and He has answered your prayers. But now it is too late, and you cannot see the gift you've been given. It won't be long before your enemies destroy you. They will muck you out like a mad mama cow and do the same to your kids. They won't leave one stone standing on top of another because you were too blind to see when God stood among you."

LUKE 19:41-44

Would you be too blind to see it if God stood among you? We'd like to say "no," but in our busyness and distractions, we miss it every single day.

As cowboys, we've spent countless hours under the open sky, but have we ever stopped to see Him in those moments? We hear the laughter of our children or grandchildren in the backyard, but have we ever invited God to enjoy that moment with us?

God is also present in the faces of those in poverty or who suffer from rejection. Jesus said, "When I was hungry, you fed Me. When I was thirsty, you gave Me a drink." When

His cowboys asked Him when they'd done that, He said, "Anything you do for the least of My children, you do it to Me."

God is among us every day. His presence is in every interaction. Let us not be blind to Him. Take time today to look around and see Him.

COWBOY CALL

Don't wait! See the gift you've been given today. Jesus came not only to save you, but also to walk alongside you in your struggles and triumphs. As you ride through the unpredictable and often demanding paths of life, remember that the ultimate gift has already been given. Accept it, cherish it, and carry it with you always.

Our goal is,

and always

should be,
oneness with God.

Authority from God

One day Jesus was teaching in the main church and telling folks about the Good News. Many church leaders and preachers came up to Him and asked, "Who said You could teach in here?" . . . So Jesus said, "If you won't answer, then neither will I."

LUKE 20:1-2,8

Good will always be accosted by evil. Spreading the Good News will mean a lot of bad people will try to stop you. It even happened to Jesus. The church leaders and preachers approached Him while He was teaching in the Temple. They were trying to bombard Jesus with questions so He would break one of their many rules, and it would give them a reason to kill Him. But Jesus didn't give them the satisfaction. He answered their question with a question that He knew they didn't want to answer. Jesus wouldn't get caught up in their games.

In order to spread the Good News or be somewhat effective in our gathering of souls for God's ranch, we have to know how to respond to our critics; and one of the best strategies Jesus employs is one that we can use as well. We don't get caught up in their games.

COWBOY CALL

I was at an elderly family member's birthday celebration, sitting across from an older woman I didn't know. We made small talk, and then she asked what I did for a living. I told her I was a preacher. I tried to hide my dismay when she said, "No, you're not." I smiled, thinking maybe she was joking, and asked, "Why do you say that?" She looked me right in the eye and said, "Because you're not old enough to be a preacher. You're barely old enough to be a man, and you have no business telling me or anyone else what God would want or not want. Who do you think gave you the right to call yourself a preacher?" I smiled and said, "If you don't know the answer to that, you wouldn't believe me if I told you." People will try to trap you with fancy words and questions. Don't fall for it. Jesus never did. Just because someone asks you a question doesn't mean you have to answer it.

Worrying and Partying All Night Long

"Be careful! Worrying about life is as bad as partying all night and coming home drunk. Don't let any of these happen to you."

LUKE 21:34

Over and over Jesus tells us that half a bubble off one way is as bad as half a bubble off the other way too. Sin is sin. It's so difficult for us to comprehend this notion. We like to categorize sins ranging from "not that big of a deal" to "deadly." But all sin is deadly.

It's deadly because it hardens our hearts. And when our hearts become hard, then we can no longer distinguish God's voice from the roar of the crowd. Remember, God speaks in a gentle whisper.

Jesus's statement here illustrates the fact that sin is sin, and it's all bad. Nobody ever thinks about worrying being just as bad as partying all night and coming home drunk. That's why John said that anyone who claims to be without sin is deceiving themselves.

Even Paul said that everyone has sinned and falls short of the glory of God (Romans 3:23). This doesn't make sin okay, but it does point out that we need saving from our sins every single day.

Be careful, though. It's easy to become sin-focused instead of Christ-focused. Jesus died once and for all for our sins. This should be our focus—to strive every single day to keep our eyes on Him.

COWBOY CALL

Luke 21:34 tells us to be on guard against the anxieties and worries of life because if we get bogged down in our worry it will distract us from what truly matters. Being in a constant state of fear can cloud our judgment, steal our peace, and lead us to make poor decisions. So stay watchful, and don't let anything get in the way of you making choices that will draw you closer to God.

When We Fail

"Pete, listen close. [s]atan has asked to rope and drag you to the fire. But I have talked to My Dad about you so that He will strengthen you in the days to come and you will be filled with courage after you fail. When you come back to Me, be there for your brothers who you ride with and encourage them."

LUKE 22:31-32

One of my quirks is that I try to never capitalize "satan." Some might call it petty, but to me, it's a constant reminder of just how little he is compared to my God.

In my journey of faith, I've come to understand the power of perspective. The devil, the adversary, may appear formidable, but through this small quirk, I choose to emphasize his insignificance in the face of the greatness of my God.

The Bible reassures us of God's supremacy. Psalm 95:3 (NASB) declares, "For the LORD is a great God and a great King above all gods." Ephesians 1:21–22 echoes this truth, emphasizing that God is far above all powers and dominions, both in this age and in the age to come.

By intentionally not capitalizing satan's name, I'm making a statement. I'm reminding myself, and anyone who notices, that our God reigns supreme. He's greater, stronger, and more victorious than any adversary we may face.

This perspective empowers me to stand firm in my faith. It strengthens me to resist the enemy's tactics, knowing that his power is limited in comparison to the boundless power and love of my heavenly Father.

So, let us embrace this quirk as a symbol of the enormous gap between our God and satan. May it serve as a constant reminder that we can face life's challenges with confidence, knowing that our God is infinitely greater. He is the Source of our strength and the Bringer of ultimate victory.

COWBOY CALL

It's not a question of if we fail, but when. For some of us, it seems like we fail on the daily. For others, it may be a little harder to see sometimes, but it happens. It happened to Pete. It'll happen to us. But I don't think the focus should be on *how we fail* as much as it should be on *how to saddle back up*. Jesus asked His Father to give Pete courage after he failed. The courage to get back on the horse again doesn't come from us—it comes from God. This usually comes in the form of knowing that you should get back on, and I'm really not talking about horses. Jesus then tells Pete what to do after failing. He said to be there for others. We should do the same.

The Torn Curtain

Now the sun was standing directly overhead, but a darkness descended over the land for about three hours. The sun seemed to have lost its light. At the same time, the curtain that symbolized the separation of God from man, which hung in the main church, was torn from the top to the bottom. With the last of His strength, Jesus said, "Dad, I give My life into Your hands." When He'd spoke these words, His final breath left His body.

LUKE 23:44-46

The Holy of Holies was the section of the Temple that housed the Ark of the Covenant (a gold-plated wooden chest that housed the two tablets bearing the Ten Commandments) and allowed God to appear on earth. The curtain that separated the Holy of Holies from the rest of the Temple was sixty feet tall and four inches thick. That's more like a wall of fabric than a curtain.

So, why was the tearing of the curtain such a big deal? Well, annually the high priest went into the Holy of Holies to atone, or make amends, for the sins of God's people by sprinkling the blood of sacrificial animals and offering incense. When the curtain was torn, it ended the need for the high priest to continue offering sacrifices. The final Sacrifice (Jesus) had been made, and it would last for all time.

Since the curtain was torn from top to bottom, this meant *God* did the tearing. He was saying no more sacrifices were needed because Jesus Himself was now seated at His right hand to atone for our sins. Now each one of us has direct access to the Father, meaning we don't have to pray through anybody else. We don't have to confess our sins through anybody else. We can go directly to God for what we need.

COWBOY CALL

When God tore the veil, He was saying that He wanted to connect with us. He no longer wanted to be separated from us—He got rid of all the barriers and invited us to approach Him with confidence. What a privilege to go to the Father! What a gift! Are you taking advantage of this connection? Are you talking to your Father in heaven? Take a moment today to talk to God and thank Him for removing everything that stood in the way of you and Him connecting.

A Dead Run

The cowboys scoffed at the idea of such a thing and didn't believe a word of it. But Pete had to see for himself. He ran to the tomb and looked. All that was inside was the linen cloth. He went back and wondered what had happened to Jesus.

LUKE 24:11-12

In our world today, we want evidence, facts, and figures before we believe anything. However, in our spiritual journey, God calls us to develop faith—a belief in what we cannot see, touch, or prove.

Hebrews 11:1 defines *faith* as "being full of hope and plumb certain of what lies over the hill that we cannot see." This verse beautifully encapsulates the essence of faith; it's not about visible proof, but about *invisible certainty*. Faith believes God's promises, His goodness, and His love, even when it can't see them standing in the pen.

Jesus Himself emphasizes the importance of faith. In John 20:29, He says to Thomas, "You say that now that you've seen Me. Better blessings await the cowboy who believes without seeing." Clearly, faith isn't about seeing, but about believing. It's about trusting God in the midst of uncertainties, storms, and trials.

But faith isn't just a passive acceptance; it's an active trust in God. It's a choice to believe in His promises even when circumstances seem contrary. It's choosing to trust Him when we cannot trace His hand or see His steps in the dirt. Faith is the cinch that holds our saddle on while we ride and rope.

In a world that demands proof, we need to strive to grow in our faith. Let us remember that although we may not have physical evidence of God's existence, we have the assurance of His unfailing love, His unwavering promises, and His unchanging character.

COWBOY CALL

When Pete hears the news that Jesus has risen from the dead, he takes off to see for himself. He doesn't walk; he runs! When Pete sees Jesus another time, he jumps out of the boat and swims to shore instead of waiting for the boat to get there. There's a lot we can learn from that. We shouldn't be lazy about getting to Jesus. We aren't usually standing there out of breath waiting for the doors of the church to open on Sunday. We don't rush home from work to read the Scriptures. We aren't quick to hit our knees in prayer. Have you become lazy in your faith? Don't wait any longer. Run as fast as you can to the foot of the cross and have your sins forgiven.

Offered a Chance

At this time, the real Light was riding down from heaven to join us here on earth. He had come down to ride in the pastures that He had made. But the world He created did not recognize Him. He rode straight to His people, but they shunned Him and turned Him away. But because of His love, He offered the chance for every cowboy and cowgirl to become one of God's kids just by believing in Him. When a cowboy becomes one of God's kids, nothing really happens to him physically. The transformation occurs in his soul. He is branded and marked for eternity by God Himself.

JOHN 1:9-13

In this ride of faith with God, a momentous change occurs when we accept Christ as our Lord and Savior. John 1:12 says, "But because of His love, He offered the chance for every cowboy and cowgirl to become one of God's kids just by believing in Him." Through faith in Jesus Christ, we're adopted into God's family and we gain a new identity as God's child. As recipients of His love, grace, mercy, and blessings, we're heirs to His Kingdom, given the promise of eternal life. We're given a new purpose, to ride for His glory and share His love with others.

This trail challenges us to grow and mature spiritually. As God's children, we're called to reflect His character—to exhibit love, kindness, patience, and forgiveness. We obey Him, follow His commands, and walk in His ways. It's a journey of transformation where we're continually shaped and molded into Christ's likeness. As we walk with God and abide, or remain, in His Word, we become more like Him—loving what He loves, hating what He hates, and truly seeking to do His will.

COWBOY CALL

I was fortunate to spend most of my high school years on a big ranch in West Texas. I know many people wish they'd had that opportunity. But let me tell you, it wasn't all skittles and unicorns. I have hundreds of stories of getting bucked off, kicked, stomped, and scared out of my mind. Similarly, Jesus offers us all a chance to work on His outfit. He makes the offer, but He doesn't force the taking of it. When we read Scripture, we hear of the marvelous rewards that are associated with riding for His brand, but we also read of the sacrifice and heartache that will accompany it. In the end, I'll tell you it was all worth it. Every single moment on the ranches I've worked has made me stronger, but they've also made me realize my weaknesses. God offers us the same chance. Will you take the chance that has been offered?

Do What Your Mama Tells You

The next day, Jesus attended a wedding in Cana with His mom. Jesus's twelve cowboys were also invited to the party. The celebration ran out of wine before the party was over, and Jesus's mom said, "They've run out of wine."

"That ain't none of My business," Jesus replied. "I'm staying out of the limelight for now, but My time will come."

But Mary was undaunted, and she told the serving staff, "Do whatever He tells you to do."

JOHN 2:1-5

In our connected world, where information is constantly at our fingertips, it can be tempting to stick your nose where it really doesn't belong. However, Scripture reminds us of the importance of minding our own business in I Thessalonians 4:11, where Paul instructs, "Make it your top priority to lead a quiet life. You do this by minding your own business and working like a cowboy should. You've already heard this from us, so this isn't anything new."

This doesn't mean we should be indifferent toward others; in fact, we are called to assist others in their times of need, to come alongside them when they are struggling. But there are other times when we need to respect personal boundaries and focus on our own spiritual growth and responsibilities. Jesus illustrated this principle in John 21:21–22, when Peter asked about John's future: "When Pete saw him [John], he asked, 'What about this cowboy? What will happen to him, Lord?' Jesus said, 'If I want to keep him alive until the day I return, it is none of your business. You just follow Me and don't worry about anything else.'" Essentially, Jesus was telling Peter to focus on his own journey and not to compare or concern himself with others.

So, when we see an opportunity to insert ourselves into other people's lives, let's ask God to guide us in our responses. Sometimes we need to strive to mind our own business, focusing on our own walk with God, and trust that He is perfectly capable of handling everyone else's. But . . . there is an exception. You do the business that your mama tells you to.

COWBOY CALL

This is one the most famous stories in the Bible, when Jesus turns water into wine. But I've always been intrigued by the boldness of Mary. Look at how Jesus responds to His mother's "request" for help. He said it's not any of His business. It makes me laugh out loud that she completely dismissed His statement and told the staff to do whatever Jesus said to do. Even Jesus didn't cross His mama. He did what she asked.

Old Saint Nick

There was a Jewish leader and Pharisee named Nicodemus, or Nick for short. He didn't want anyone to see him talking to Jesus, so one evening after dark, he sought Him out and said, "Hey, Boss, we all know You are from God because of the miracles You can do." But Jesus said, "I'm telling you the truth, unless you are born again, you will never see the inside of God's ranch."

JOHN 3:1-3

Being born again is a fundamental concept in Christianity; it's a spiritual rebirth that signifies a transformation in Christ. Jesus Himself introduced this concept in John 3:3, when He told Nicodemus, "I'm telling you the truth, unless you are born again, you will never see the inside of God's ranch." This concept represents the transformative power of accepting Christ and His redemptive work in our lives.

Being born again means experiencing a spiritual rebirth, a transition from a life ruled by sin to a ride ruled by the Spirit of God. It's not about a physical rebirth, nor is it about self-improvement or moral reform. It's a complete transformation that only God can bring about in a person's life.

The process requires surrendering and offering our lives to Jesus, admitting that we're sorry sinners in need of a Savior. It's only through faith in Him that we can be born again and start a new life—a life guided by His Word, His love, and His purpose for us.

Second Corinthians 5:17 vividly illustrates this transformation: “This means that anyone who rides for the Lord has become a brand-new cowboy. The old city life is gone and a new life of purpose has begun.” When we are born again, we become a brand-new cowboy—a brand-new creation in Christ.

COWBOY CALL

Nick didn’t want anyone seeing him talking to Jesus because he belonged to the group known as the Pharisees. They get a bad rap, but that doesn’t mean they were all bad people. I think there was just a lot of peer pressure for the group to hold on to their lofty positions of power. They didn’t even want to relinquish the stage to the Son of God! Nick went under the cover of night so no one would see him talking to Jesus. Similarly, we might only talk about Jesus in Bible studies and on Sunday mornings, where it’s safe and our friends won’t see us. Don’t be ashamed to be seen with Jesus. We can be seen riding with Him by sharing our faith with others, by praying with those in need, and by the way we act in public.

Lipstick on a Pig

Jesus smiled as He kneeled down by the well and said, "Anyone who drinks this water will eventually get thirsty again. But the water I give is a fountain of youth and gives eternal life."
The woman quickly said, "I would take Your water in a heartbeat. That way I wouldn't have to walk all the way out here to get water every day."
"Go get your husband," Jesus told her.
"I don't have one," the woman replied sheepishly.
Jesus said, "I think you're putting lipstick on a pig. Truth is, you have had five husbands and the man you live with now ain't one of them. So, you're right. You don't have a husband."

JOHN 4:13-18

When Jesus speaks of "living water" in John 4:14, He introduces a rich metaphor that illustrates His role as the Source of eternal life. He tells the Samaritan woman at the well, "Anyone who drinks this water will eventually get thirsty again. But the water I give is a fountain of youth and gives eternal life."

Here, "living water" symbolizes the Holy Spirit, eternal life, and the spiritual nourishment that only Jesus can provide. Just as water is essential for our physical survival, the living water of Christ is crucial for our spiritual survival.

Without it, our souls become parched and lifeless. We become a dry pond with weeds and hog wallers.

Jesus offers a well of life that never runs dry—spiritual nourishment that quenches all our desires and needs. This living water represents the divine grace, love, and mercy that flow from Jesus to all who believe in Him. It cleanses us from our sins, refreshes our spirits, and imparts eternal life. The Holy Spirit resides in us, guiding us, empowering us, and constantly renewing us, transforming us from the inside out.

COWBOY CALL

The woman at the well is another famous story in the Bible. The woman Jesus talked to was a Samaritan woman (a half-blood Jew). Samaritans had married outside of the Jewish people and were vastly shunned by full-blooded Jews. The woman was seen as "unclean," an outcast among her own people. Just the fact that Jesus was talking to her alone at the well was scandalous. She was a Samaritan and a sinner at that. She was living with a man who wasn't her husband. Despite knowing all this, Jesus encourages her with the love of God. He both confronts her about her sin and comforts her with the truth of the Gospel. This breaks through her hard heart; as a result, many others are brought to meet Christ.

*It takes gumption
to leave behind
what's comfortable*

and take
a step toward
a different way.

The Danger of Approval

"Make no mistake, your approval means diddly-squat to Me. I see into your hearts and know that you do not ride for God. I have been sent by My Father, and you turn Me away. I have come saying, 'Look at God,' and you reject Me. Others have come saying, 'Look at me,' and you welcome them. No wonder y'all can't believe. You're too busy standing in a big circle patting each other on the back. You seek glory from each other instead of from God."

JOHN 5:41-44

The Bible warns us about the dangers of vanity and self-centeredness, and one of the clearest examples is found in Proverbs 16:18: "How much can a cowboy boast when he chokes to death on his own pride?" In our society, it's easy to fall into the trap of vanity and self-centeredness. We're often encouraged to focus on our own achievements, looks, and success. But this leads us away from God and into a destructive cycle of self-worship.

Vanity and self-centeredness are forms of idolatry. When we become overly focused on ourselves, we replace God with our own image. We start to believe that we're self-sufficient and don't need God. This is a dangerous lie because apart from God, we can do nothing (John 15:5).

Being consumed with ourselves also blinds us to the needs of others. Jesus taught us to love our neighbors as ourselves (Mark 12:31), but vanity makes this command hard to follow. It's difficult to extend love, kindness, and compassion to others when we're so focused on ourselves.

COWBOY CALL

Who doesn't want approval? We all do. It feels good to feel approved of. But the danger of seeking approval is that it's addictive. We start doing things for the approval of others instead of for God. Instead of being truthful, we say things to gain approval. Seeking the approval of God means oftentimes that you will incur the wrath of man. You can't have both the approval of man and the approval of God—at least not entirely or often. What have you been doing that is approval seeking? How many decisions do you honestly make that are decided on the approval or disapproval of someone besides God?

ONLY ONE THING

They all replied, "We want to rope, ride, and brand for God's outfit too. What do we have to do first to saddle up with Ya?" Jesus said, "There is only one thing you have to do. Give your whole life to the Top Hand that God has sent ya."

JOHN 6:28-29

In Matthew 11:30, Jesus declares, "Ridin' for Me is easy, and workin' for Me ain't hard either." It's a beautiful reminder that following God doesn't have to be complicated or burdensome.

Many times, we complicate our walk with God by setting unrealistic expectations for ourselves, tying hard and fast to legalistic traditions, or trying to earn God's love and acceptance. We burden ourselves with guilt, worry, and fear, thinking that we're being faithful followers of Christ. However, these self-imposed trials are not from God and only make our ride with Christ more difficult.

God doesn't want us to strive or struggle in our relationship with Him. He desires a relationship based on grace, love, and freedom. Our faith journey isn't about following a set of rigid rules or achieving spiritual perfection. It's about riding with God daily, trusting Him, and surrendering to His will. We're called to rest in His grace, live by His Word, and love as Jesus loved.

When we simplify our faith and focus on God's grace, we find that our walk with God becomes less burdensome and more joyful. Let's pray for the wisdom to keep our faith simple, grounded in God's love and grace, making our ride with Him, and for Him, a delightful and fulfilling experience.

COWBOY CALL

I think we have vastly diluted what it means to give your life to Christ. The "altar call" is often a substitution for joining a church. We get baptized as a requirement instead of as a symbol of our identification and relation to Jesus's death, burial, and resurrection. Maybe giving our whole life to God would be better understood as "swearing absolute and total allegiance to the Man and mission of Jesus Christ" . . . and not just until Sunday service is over, but until your life is. Our total allegiance to Jesus means that we live our lives like He did. We obey Him in the way He said to do things and ride the whole trail He blazed. Without obeying the Word of God, we might as well be riding a stick horse, waving our hats in the air, and yelling, "Yeehaw." Jesus's mission was to tell everyone that eternal life is granted only through His sacrifice. We share in that mission of telling others the Good News. Are you all in or hardly in at all?

They Laughed at Him

Then Nicodemus, the Pharisee who had met with Jesus before, spoke up and asked, "Does our Law convict a man before his side of the story is told?" They laughed at him and said, "Are you a Podunk from Galilee, too? Search the Good Book, and you will see that no prophet ever comes from Galilee."

JOHN 7:50-52

The Bible teaches us the importance of standing up for others, especially those who are vulnerable or marginalized. In Proverbs 31:8–9, we're instructed, "Defend those who cannot defend themselves and stand up for those who cannot stand up for themselves. Speak up and speak fairly. Defend the rights of everyone, especially the poor and needy."

Jesus Christ exemplified this principle throughout His ministry on earth. He defended the weak, comforted the oppressed, and reached out to the marginalized. He extended love, mercy, and compassion to all, no matter their social status or background.

As followers of Christ, we're called to do the same. We're called to be a voice for the voiceless and a defender of the defenseless. We're supposed to stand up against injustice and unrighteousness, not out of self-righteousness or pride, but out of love and compassion for our fellow human beings.

This takes a heap of courage, humility, and wisdom. It requires us to step out of our comfort zones, or as I like to call them, our "sissy pens," to risk ridicule or rejection, and to love others as Christ loved us. It may not be easy, but it's a foundational part of our Christian ride.

COWBOY CALL

Nicodemus found some courage and spoke up. And look where it got him. They laughed at him. But I believe it was worth it. Nick stood up for Jesus in a crowd of his peers and colleagues. He knew what he was going to say was not going to be received well at all. And yet, Nick found the willpower to overcome his hesitation, and he spoke out against his peers and colleagues. The next time you have the chance, will you find the courage to see the truth even if it means people laugh at you?

SEEING THE TRUTH

"Where is your Father then?" they replied.
"Let's hear what He has to say."
Jesus said, "If you don't recognize who I am,
how can you recognize who My Father is? If
you knew Me, you would know Him."

JOHN 8:19

John 8:31–32 says, "Jesus spoke then to those who believed. '*You ride for Me if you do what I tell you to do. Only then will you know the truth, and the truth will set you free.*'" This powerful statement gives us the promise of freedom in truth—a truth that comes only from knowing and understanding God's Word.

We may often find ourselves all tangled up in the world's confusion, struggling to figure out what's genuinely true in a storm of misinformation and dealing from the bottom of the deck. In times like these, we must remember that God is the ultimate Source of all truth.

Jesus Christ, the Son of God, is referred to as "the way, and the truth, and the life" in John 14:6 (NASB). Therefore, seeking truth means seeking Christ, immersing ourselves in His teachings, seeking His wisdom, and striving to ride as He has taught us.

The truth of Christ is not just an abstract idea, but a life-changing reality. It's a truth that brings clarity in confusion, hope in despair, and freedom to ride for the Brand. It's a truth that transforms us, guides us, and empowers us to live a life that's pleasing to God.

COWBOY CALL

In John 8:19, Jesus was talkin' to a bunch of folks who didn't quite understand who He was. They were questionin' Him, askin' where His Father was. And this is where we find out that Jesus is the Doorway to God. If we truly know Jesus, we know our heavenly Father too. This is so important because it clarifies Jesus's role as the Bridge between us and God, and it shows that Jesus is not just a wise teacher or prophet (as other religions believe), but the Son of God, fully divine.

Ridin' for the Brand

As they rode along, Jesus saw a man who had been blind his whole life. "Boss," His cowboys asked, "why is this man blind? Did his daddy commit some kind of sin that made God mad or something?" "Neither of his parents did anything to make this happen," Jesus said as He dismounted. "This happened so God could show y'all what He can do. While the sun is shining, the Son will be out shinin': ropin', gatherin', doctorin', and brandin'. It's what My Daddy sent Me to do. But it'll be dark soon, and no one will be able to work. While I am here, I am the light that lets people see."

JOHN 9:1-5

In Ephesians 2:10, Paul tells us, "Like the greatest saddle maker ever, we were tooled by God Himself, created in Christ Jesus to do good things God prepared for us before we even got here."

This Scripture beautifully illustrates our purpose in riding for Christ. Our purpose is not merely to exist, but to serve, to love, and to be cowboys who bring God's grace and mercy to a world that desperately needs it. God intricately designed each one of us with unique talents, abilities, and spiritual gifts—not for our glory, but for His. Our purpose is to use these gifts to serve others, spread the Gospel, gather the lost, and bring glory to God's name.

Sometimes, finding our purpose may seem difficult, but we must remember that our ultimate purpose is to glorify God, reflect the love and grace of Christ, and be His hands and feet in this world. It may come in simple acts of kindness, in sharing God's Word, or in serving in our local church or community.

COWBOY CALL

Jesus is the Top Hand in His Daddy's outfit. Jesus said that as long as the sun was shining, He'd be out there shining too. But what did He mean by "shining"? Jesus would be out there roping people in with the truth. That's the whole reason we rope: to make sure cattle don't get away. Jesus said He'd be out there gathering. We gather cattle so we can work them. Jesus does the same with us. He also said He'd be doctoring and branding. He came to heal the sick and brand those with the promise of adoption into His Father's family. Are you still throwing your head up and running off to brush up?

Day Workers

"I am the Good Cowboy. The Good Cowboy will die for His cattle. The day worker is not the cowboy and does not own the cattle. If a day worker sees a wolf or a rustler, he's not going to defend the cattle with his life. He will hightail it out of there. Then the herd is run through the fence and scattered. The day worker isn't going to put his life on the line."

JOHN 10:11-13

In the passage above, Jesus declared, "I am the Good Cowboy. The Good Cowboy will die for His cattle." This profound statement speaks volumes about the protective nature of Christ toward us, His cowboys.

Just as a cowboy watches over his cattle, Jesus watches over us with an unwavering awareness. His protection isn't a result of our good deeds or righteousness or how well we rope; it's because of His unlimited love and grace toward us. Even in the face of danger, Jesus, our Good Cowboy, has proven His love by laying down His life on the cross for our sins.

Every day we encounter various trials and tribulations. We may feel overwhelmed, vulnerable, and even afraid. But remember, Jesus assures us, "I've told you all of this so you will be able to be calm. While you ride for Me, you'll have plenty of trouble, but keep your chin up! I have conquered this world" (John 16:33).

Christ's protection doesn't mean that we won't face mad mama cows and rank bulls, but it ensures that we won't face them alone. He is with us in every storm and every wreck, guiding us, strengthening us, and providing us with the grace we need to endure.

COWBOY CALL

Jesus is also saying in these verses that He didn't come here for a part-time, weekend gig. He came to give His life for those He loves. Now, that's what I call loyalty. We need to ask ourselves the same question: Are we in this for a weekend gig? Are we just trying to get the good stuff, or are we willing to give it all? Jesus didn't say He would take any part-timers to the forever pastures. He said that we had to die to ourselves in order to live (Luke 9:23). Most people who say they believe in God—or those who just go to church on Sundays—aren't willing to make the ultimate sacrifice. They don't want a full-time job. They just want a weekend gig. In what ways have you been a day worker instead of being all in?

Come Here

But Jesus responded, "Didn't you hear Me say that if you believed you would see the glory of God?" So they rolled the stone aside, and Jesus looked into heaven and said, "Dad, thank You for always hearing Me when I call. I don't have to talk out loud for You to hear Me, but I say this for the benefit of all who are listening. I want them to believe in You and Me." Then Jesus stated in a commanding voice, "Lazarus, come here!" And the dead guy walked out of the tomb. He was still wrapped in the burial cloth. Jesus told those standing nearby, "Take off his grave clothes. He won't need them anymore."

JOHN 11:40-44

My wife has a bunch of chickens, and one day a dog that we were keeping for a friend while they were out of town decided chicken was on the menu.

I looked up and saw this dog, who had been out among the chickens for three days without incident, killing one of my wife's favorites. They were young chickens, and she'd raised them by hand. Oh, and she was out of town. That makes it worse. They were my responsibility.

I made the dog spit out the chicken. I laid the poor chicken's body on a table near the coop while I put the dog away.

When I went back to get the dead chicken, she was gone. My other three dogs were on the back deck, so where did this dead chicken go? I looked everywhere, and then I found her. She was eating with the others. I'll admit, I didn't really check for a heartbeat after what I'd witnessed, but there she was, walking around.

I'm not kidding that I yelled, "Lazarus! Come forth!" That's her name still today . . . and she's doing just fine.

COWBOY CALL

How many times did your dad have to tell you to come here? When a parent speaks to their child, most of the time the kid does what he is told. I've always been fascinated that Jesus's command to "come here" was heard even across the realm of death. There's nothing that can stand in the way of the power of God. If Lazarus could hear the command of Jesus to walk out of his grave, what excuse do we—who are dead in our transgressions—have for not obeying His same order? Jesus said, "Come to Me," and we should listen.

Quit Your Whinin'

"Right now I feel like I'm hung up in the stirrup, but do you think I'm going to whine about it and say, 'Make it stop, Dad'? No, this is what I came to do. God, all this glory is Yours!" Then a mighty voice came from heaven, "I have shown My power, and I will do so again." Everyone was looking around to see where the voice came from. Some said it was thunder and others said an angel had spoken.

JOHN 12:27–29

Riding for Jesus means surrendering our own desires, taking up our crosses, and walking the path that He walked. This journey isn't without wrecks and challenges, and sometimes the cost may seem too high . . . but the reward is eternal.

The world often presents tempting alternatives to riding for the Brand. Comfort, popularity, and earthly success can seem appealing, but they're fleeting. As Christians, we're called to prioritize our relationship with Jesus over worldly pursuits, even when it means facing ridicule, rejection, or persecution.

Riding for the Brand may mean swimming against the current of societal norms, standing for truth when it's unpopular, and loving even when it's difficult. It may mean losing friendships, opportunities, or status. But the apostle

Paul reminds us, "The only thing in life that is important is knowing Jesus Christ as my Lord. Because of Him, I have left everything behind. I left my former life like garbage waiting on the fly-wagon. You have to lose everything if you are to gain Christ" (Philippians 3:8).

COWBOY CALL

Have you ever felt like you're hung up in the stirrup of life? You may be feeling that way right now. I'm willing to bet that, like me, more than once in your life you've whined to God and asked Him to take away your pain. Jesus knew what He lived for. He came to this earth to do for us what we couldn't do for ourselves. He came to live a perfect life and then be sacrificed for our sins. He never whined about it. He never blamed anyone or felt sorry for Himself.

I wish I could say the same for us. But you know what? God never wastes our pain. He uses it to help others, and when that happens, He's glorified. Pain makes our faith stronger if we don't give up. And especially if we don't whine about it.

True Humility

They were eating the evening meal, and Judas had already made his deal with the devil. The plan was already in motion to double-cross Jesus. . . . Jesus got up from the table, took off His clothes [or His "outer clothing"], and wrapped a towel around His waist. He poured water in a big bowl and started washing His cowboys' feet. He dried their feet with the towel He had wrapped around His waist.
When He got to Pete, Pete said, "I ain't gonna let You lower Yourself on my account. You ain't washin' my feet, Boss."
Jesus looked up and said, "You don't understand what I'm doing right now, but one day you will."
"It ain't gonna happen," Pete said. "I won't let You touch my nasty feet."
Then Jesus said, "Then you don't ride for Me."

JOHN 13:2, 4-8

Betrayal is a painful experience we all encounter at some point in our lives. Whether it's from a close friend, family member, or trusted pard, the sting of betrayal can leave us feeling wounded and alone. However, as Christians, we can find comfort in knowing that Jesus, too, experienced betrayal.

Judas Iscariot, one of Jesus's twelve disciples, agreed to betray Jesus in exchange for thirty silver coins. Despite this,

Jesus responded not with hatred or vengeance, but with love, teaching us a valuable lesson on dealing with betrayal.

When faced with betrayal, our first instinct may be to retaliate or harbor resentment. However, Ephesians 4:31–32 reminds us, "There's no place in your saddlebags for backbiting, rage, gossip, harsh talk, or anything else that will bring dishonor to God. There is a place, though, for being kind, gentle, and forgiving, just as God has forgiven you through Jesus."

In dealing with betrayal, let's look to Jesus as our example. Let's choose to forgive, just as He has forgiven us, and let's choose to love, even when it hurts. By doing this, we not only release ourselves from the chains of bitterness, but we also demonstrate the love of Christ to those who've hurt us.

COWBOY CALL

In a time when many leaders think they're above the ones they lead, Jesus showed what real leadership looks like: humility. As a matter of fact, leadership without humility isn't leadership at all; it's prideful and tyrannical. If we truly care about those underneath us, we will be more than willing to do whatever it takes to make them better. If Jesus was willing to humble Himself for His men, we should do the same thing.

Trying to look
like a big shot
will get you
shot down,

but putting
yourself last is
the quickest way
to come in first.

Finding the Trail Home

"Don't let this get you down. Trust God and trust Me. My Father's outfit has many ranches. If that wasn't the case, would I have told you I'm going to prepare one for you? If I go to get your ranch ready, I'll come back and get you when the time is right. Then you'll be with Me forever. Y'all know the trail that leads where I'm headed."
Tom said, "Boss, we ain't sure where You're going. So how can we know which trail to take?"
Jesus said, "I am the Trail, the Truth, and the Life. No one gets to God without going through Me. If you know Me, you know My Dad. Not only that, but if you've seen Me, you've seen Him."

JOHN 14:1-7

At times, we step in the gopher hole of depending solely on our abilities, even when it comes to our salvation. We toil, strive, and aim to gain God's approval by our deeds. Yet, the Bible clarifies in Titus 3:5, "He saved us, not because we'd done something good, but because He did it all perfect and had mercy on our souls."

Truthfully, our salvation isn't something we can earn or attain. It's a gift from God, freely given through the sacrifice of Jesus Christ. Our salvation isn't a reward of our deeds, but a result of His abundant grace and our faith in Jesus.

Trusting can be a struggle, particularly when we're accustomed to controlling situations. But when we entrust our salvation to Jesus, we recognize our inability to save ourselves. We embrace His sacrifice, His grace, and His love. We let go of our control and surrender our lives to the One who loved us so much to give His life for us.

COWBOY CALL

One of the impossible things to figure out on our own is where the trail is that leads to heaven. You can't find the trail without Jesus. There's no back door or road signs. You must follow Jesus. What this means is that you have to know Him, trust Him, follow Him, and obey Him. There's no other way. While we do follow the same God, we each have an individual trail marked out. While we can learn from each other about how to listen and follow Him, the journey is one we must take for ourselves.

I Came and Found You

"Y'all didn't come and find Me, I came and found you. I taught y'all how to make a difference in the world . . . a difference that will last. Anything y'all need will be given to you if you ask. Don't forget what I've told you to do—love each other."

JOHN 15:16-17

In Matthew 7:7–8, Jesus says, "If you need somethin', keep tellin' the Boss about it and you will get it. If you keep lookin' for the cows in the pasture, you will find them if you don't give up. If you keep knockin' on the barn door, He will open it for you. If you ask, you will receive. If you knock, the door will be opened. If you look, you will find." This Scripture shows God's willingness to provide for our needs when we ask Him in faith.

But it's important to remember that this promise doesn't mean we'll always receive exactly what we want. Rather, God promises to provide what we need, which may not always align with our desires. As our heavenly Father, He knows our true needs far better than we do.

Jesus reiterated this promise when He said in John 15:7, "If you ride with Me, and I ride with you, I'll help you with anything you ask." Here Jesus emphasizes the importance of abiding in Him, which means resting, trusting, and being aligned with God and His Word. Abiding in Jesus is riding with Jesus. It means spending time in His presence through prayer and studying His Word. It's doing what He says the way He says to do it. It's loving others as He has loved us.

When we abide in Christ, our wants align with His. We start to desire what He desires for us. And when we ask according to His will, we can be assured that He will answer.

COWBOY CALL

There's an old joke of how a drunk man stumbled on a river baptism ceremony. The preacher hollered out to him and asked him if he wanted to find Jesus. The man said he did and waded out to the preacher. The preacher dunked him under the water, and as the man came up, he was asked if he'd found Jesus. He said no. The preacher dunked him several more times, and each time he was asked if he'd found Jesus; the answer was always no. Finally, the exasperated preacher asked what the problem was. The drunk slurred in return, "Are you sure He's down there?"

We don't find Jesus. Jesus finds us. It's a beautiful moment when we realize the presence of Christ in our life, not because we have suddenly found Him, but because He sought us out.

The Work of the Holy Spirit

"But now I'm about to head out. Every one of you is missing the point about where I'm going. If you understood, you would be happy, but yet you do nothing except hang your heads. Truth is, it's a good thing I'm going. The Trail Guide can't come and help you until I'm gone. When He gets here, He's gonna show people three things: sin, being right with God, and the judgment that waits for unbelievers. The world's greatest sin is that they do not believe in who I am. Y'all are going to be made right with God when I get to Him. I won't be around anymore, but I'll still be with you. Judgment awaits those who follow the world because its ruler has already been judged."

JOHN 16:5-11

I have this weird way of looking at death. I believe that we aren't a body that has a soul; we're a soul trapped in a mortal body. Our natural place to be is with our Creator, not here without Him. I think our souls long to be with Jesus, but as long as the prison's power source is working, we must stay here.

What's the power source of our prison? It's our heart. As long as our heart's beating, as long as our lungs need to be filled with air, as long as our brain functions to keep our prison alive, we'll have to endure this world.

I say this because Jesus said that His cowboys were missing the point about His death. As ironic as it sounds, Jesus's death was the best thing that ever happens to this world. And when we're finally set free from this mortal prison, it will be the best thing that ever happens to us.

But understand, we aren't in prison because we did something wrong; we're working undercover trying to free others who are held captive to sin. It's our duty to point the way to freedom to all.

COWBOY CALL

The Holy Spirit's job is to show us the sin in our lives. Deep inside, we know the things we do that are against God's ways. The Holy Spirit also shows us the way to righteousness. That's a fancy word for being right with God. There's only one way to be right with God, and that's through giving our whole life to the Man and mission of Jesus Christ. There are other things the Holy Spirit does in our lives, but without these foundational things, we're unable to accept the power and wisdom that come from Him.

Stuck Here for a While Longer

"Everything I have is yours, and everything you have is Mine. These cowboys have honored Me. I'm headed home, but they will be stuck here for a while longer. Holy Father, keep them safe by the power of Your name, and the power of the name You gave Me. That way they can be as close as Me and You."

JOHN 17:10-11

Deepening our fellowship (or our ride) with God is a journey that begins with a simple, yet profound step: accepting Jesus Christ as our Lord and Savior. However, creating this relationship requires intentionality and commitment. It's about nurturing a heart-to-heart connection that goes beyond rituals and religion and affects every area of our lives.

James 4:8 says, "Spread your bedroll next to the Boss, and He will keep the fire warm and the wolves away. Wash your hands of the filth you've been living in and quit ridin' for the Boss during the day and the devil by night." This Scripture highlights the partnership of our relationship with God. He's always ready and willing to ride close to us, but we also have a part to play.

To draw near to God, we need to consistently spend time in His presence, studying His Word, praying, and listening. As we immerse ourselves in His Word, we discover His character, promises, and ways of doing things. Through prayer, we pour out our hearts to Him, expressing our feelings, desires, and especially our doubts and fears.

Moreover, having fellowship with God involves obedience. In John 14:23, Jesus said, "The world does not love Me. You've gotta love Me to be part of My crew. Anyone who is a part of My crew will do what I've told them to do." Our obedience to God's commandments proves our love for Him and deepens our fellowship with Him. As we do these things, we experience His presence in a more real and impactful way.

COWBOY CALL

While Jesus was praying for His cowboys, He acknowledged that they would be stuck here awhile without Him. He asked God to keep them safe. Does that mean God will keep us from having hard days? No. Does that mean that we'll never get sick or hurt? No. Does that mean we won't be killed for our faith? No. Jesus was asking God to keep our souls safe. This means that when any eventuality occurs, our eternal lives are safe and secure in Christ.

Set Free

Jesus said, "I already told you that I AM He. I've asked you twice who you are looking for. You are looking for one man. Let the rest of these cowboys go." This happened because Jesus had said, "I will not lose a single one You have given Me." Then Pete swung into action. He drew his sword and cut off the ear of Malchus, the head preacher's slave. But Jesus hollered at Pete and said, "Holster your weapon, cowboy. I have to finish the job My Father gave Me. Even the suffering that goes with it."

JOHN 18:8-11

When Jesus says,"I have to finish the job My Father gave Me," He knows His earthly journey is about to end with suffering. And He moved forward with it anyway because it was God's will.

Many of us are great at starting things: new resolutions, new projects, or new commitments. Yet the true test of our faith isn't in the starting, but in the finishing. It's easy to be enthusiastic at the beginning, when everything is new and exciting. However, when the new wears off, the challenge sets in, or the process takes longer than expected, we can be tempted to give up.

The Bible encourages us to be finishers. Hebrews 12:1 tells us to "cut the hobbles of sin that are keepin' us tied down. Let us ride with strength and power in the gatherin' we've been called to." Perseverance is the key to finishing. It means staying the course, standing firm, and not giving up, no matter what comes our way.

Moreover, we're not running this race in our own strength. Philippians 1:6 assures us that "there ain't no doubt God is going to make top hands out of all of y'all. He ain't gonna quit growing you until His work is finished and Jesus comes riding back over the hill to get us all." God, who started this work in us, is faithful to help us finish it. For in the end, it's about hearing those precious words, "Well done, good and faithful cowboy" (Matthew 25:21).

COWBOY CALL

Jewish tradition holds that when someone was a slave, their ear would be marked. Malchus's ear was probably marked in that way. When Pete cut off his ear and Jesus healed it, his ear was made whole. Tradition says that Malchus went on to become a believer and a great servant of the Church. Most of those who are touched by Christ end up giving their lives to Him. Have you?

Out in the Open

Later, Joseph from Arimathea asked Pilate if he could have Jesus's body. Joseph was a secret rider for Jesus because he was afraid of the Jews. With Pilate's permission, he took Jesus's body away. Nicodemus, the fellow that had visited Jesus under the cover of darkness, gave him a hand. He brought some stuff to put on Jesus's body for burial. They followed the Jewish custom and wrapped Jesus in a long linen cloth. There was a new tomb near the place where Jesus died, and they laid Him in it because of the Day of Preparation.

JOHN 19:38-42

Joseph of Arimathea was a member of the Sanhedrin, and Nicodemus was a Pharisee. They were secret disciples of Jesus, but in this instance, they stepped out of the shadows and made their faith known by taking the body of Jesus and burying it.

God often calls us to step out of our comfort zones or—as I like to call them—sissy pens. It may be scary, but growth and transformation rarely happen in comfortable, familiar places.

Stepping out of our sissy pens requires trust and faith in God. It involves letting go of our own understanding. Proverbs 3:5–6 says, "Let the Lord have the reins of your life and pay no mind to what you know or don't know . . .

God will blaze straight the trail of a thankful cowpuncher."

God doesn't call us to step out because He wants us to fail or flounder. Rather, He wants us to grow, experience His faithfulness in new ways, and see what He can do through us when we fully rely on Him.

Today, if God's calling you to step out of your comfort zone, pull your hat down tight and take that step in faith. Trust His promises, lean on His strength, and watch as He turns your fear into faith, your insecurity into courage, and your comfort zone into a place of growth and transformation.

COWBOY CALL

Because of their public standing, Joseph of Arimathea and Nicodemus are probably the only ones who would have been granted permission to take the body. What is your public standing? Are you in a position where you feel as if you have to hide your faith? What would happen if you took a step out of your comfort zone and spoke openly about your faith? Take some time to talk to God about how to share your faith with those around you. It may mean hosting a Bible study at your house and inviting your neighbors, or it may mean asking a struggling coworker if you can pray for them. It may be uncomfortable at first, but it is so worth it.

Believe These Things

Jesus did a whole bunch of other things while He was with His cowboys, things that are not recorded in this book. But I've written these things down that you may believe that Jesus was the Son of God, the Messiah, the Top Hand, and that by believing these things, you would have eternal life.

JOHN 20:30-31

It's natural for us as humans to put limits on things, including our understanding of God's abilities. We often view Him through the lens of our *own* capabilities, forgetting that He's limitless. In Isaiah 55:8, God says, "My thinkin' is not your thinkin', neither are your trails My trails, or your methods My methods." God is the God of the impossible. There's nothing too hard for Him. He parted the Red Sea, made the sun stand still, healed the sick, and raised the dead. Our God isn't limited by time, space, resources, or any human constraints.

When we limit what God can do, we set up barriers in our faith. We believe that our problems are bigger than His power, our challenges are stronger than His strength, and our uncertainties are beyond His understanding. This is far from the truth. In Mark 10:27, "Jesus turned to them and said, 'A cowboy who thinks he can get there on his own will never make it, but a cowboy who trusts in God and God alone will never miss the gate . . . or anything else."

Let's break down the barriers of our doubts and fears. Let's trust in God's unlimited power and unfailing love. Let's remember that He is the One who makes a way where there seems to be no way. We serve a limitless God, so let's not put any limits on what He can do in and through our lives.

COWBOY CALL

Why were the Gospels written? To encourage us to believe that Jesus was the actual Son of God. He wasn't just a good person. He wasn't just an extraordinary man. He was the Son of God, and believing anything less than that is to not know or love God at all. Jesus was the Top Hand. He came to show us how to live a life that honors God. Jesus is eternal life. There is no other way besides Him. Do you truly believe these things? How has it changed your life?

Fixing Breakfast

Jesus hollered back, "Cast your net on the right side of the boat, and I bet you'll catch something." When they did, their nets started to break because of all the fish. Then the cowboy that Jesus loved said to Pete, "Hey, it's the Lord!" Pete barely registered the words before he threw his clothes on, jumped out of the boat, and swam to shore. The others hauled the fish in and headed back to shore. When they got there, they found breakfast was waiting. Jesus had cooked them some biscuits and fish.

JOHN 21:6-9

We're called to a life of transformation. When we accept Christ as our Savior, we're reborn into a new life, leaving behind our old, sorry, and sinful ways. But the ride isn't always easy; the lure of familiar habits and old ways of living can be one of our greatest temptations.

In II Peter 2:22, the Bible warns us about the dangers of returning to our old ways: "There is truth in the old saying, 'A dog goes back to its own vomit.' Another old saying that is true is, 'A clean pig will return to the mud at the first opportunity.'" This vivid metaphor serves as a reminder that returning to our old sinful habits only leads to spiritual decay and separation from God.

God calls us to a higher standard, to a life of righteousness and holiness. We must continually renew our minds and conform to the image of Christ. Romans 12:2 says, "Quit tryin' to fit into the sorry ways of the world, but be made new by changing the way you think. Only then will you find the trail that the Boss wants you to ride."

It's important to remember that we're not alone on our ride. The Holy Spirit guides us, strengthens us, and helps us to live a life that is pleasing to God. And when we falter or fail, God's grace is sufficient for us, His power made perfect in our weakness (II Corinthians 12:9).

COWBOY CALL

This is probably my favorite story in all the Gospels. The risen Savior has come back to see His cowboys. Does He reveal Himself with the power of God? Does He command them to bow down and worship Him? Does He chew them out for going back to fishing like nothing had ever happened in the previous three years? Were they battling demons and healing the lame? No, they were fishing again. And Jesus was cooking them breakfast.

Nobody could have predicted that. This is the Jesus we worship. He didn't come to condemn, but to save and serve. What a mighty Lord we serve!

Dear Friend,

This book was prayerfully crafted with you, the reader, in mind. Every word, every sentence, every page was thoughtfully written, designed, and packaged to encourage you—right where you are this very moment. At DaySpring, our vision is to see every person experience the life-changing message of God's love. So, as we worked through rough drafts, design changes, edits, and details, we prayed for you to deeply experience His unfailing love, indescribable peace, and pure joy. It is our sincere hope that through these Truth-filled pages your heart will be blessed, knowing that God cares about you—your desires and disappointments, your challenges and dreams.

He knows. He cares. He loves you unconditionally.

BLESSINGS!
THE DAYSPRING BOOK TEAM